CENTRE FOR PENTECOSTAL THEOLOGY
NATIVE NORTH AMERICAN CONTEXTUAL
MOVEMENT SERIES

Consulting Editor
Corky Alexander

NATIVE AMERICAN CONTEXTUAL MINISTRY
MAKING THE TRANSITION

NATIVE AMERICAN CONTEXTUAL MINISTRY

MAKING THE TRANSITION

CASEY CHURCH

Edited by
Ray Martell and Sue Martell

Cherohala Press
Cleveland, Tennessee

Native American Contextual Ministry: Making the Transition
Centre for Pentecostal Theology Native North American Contextual Movement Series

Published by Cherohala Press
900 Walker ST NE
Cleveland, TN 37311
USA
email: cptpress@pentecostaltheology.org
website: www.cptpress.com

Library of Congress Control Number: 2017936104

ISBN-10: 1-935931-64-4
ISBN-13: 978-1-935931-64-5

Scripture taken from the New King James Version®. Copyright © 1982 by Thomas Nelson. Used by permission. All rights reserved.

Available at special quantity discounts when purchased in bulk by bookstores, organizations, and special-interest groups.
For more information, please e-mail cptpress@pentecostaltheology.org.

DEDICATION

James N. McKinney
(1928 – 2005)

Jim McKinney (Prairie Band Potawatomi) lived in Holton, Kansas. Jim was the 'Grandfather' (*mIsho*). Rev. McKinney received degrees in theology and religious education from Midwestern Baptist Theological Seminary in Kansas City, MO. He retired from ministry in the United Methodist Church in June 1997. After that he devoted himself to revitalizing the Potawatomi language. He co-taught a class on Potawatomi language and culture at Iowa State University. Jim was one of the 'those who know' the language fluently (*nake'ndumwajek*). He was raised on the reservation in a household where both Potawatomi and English were spoken.

I owe Jim a debt of gratitude for his influence and encouragement. He guided me toward becoming the Native Christian man Creator made me to be.

– Casey Church

CONTENTS

CONTENTS

PREFACE

Preserving a Classic Car

Restoring a classic car is a hobby many men can relate to with enthusiasm. By using the example of preserving your first car – or a classic car, I will illustrate a way to lead us into the topic of change in your church.

I was born in 1957. During this era, several makes and models of automobiles now considered prized classics came on the market. When new, these automobiles handled and performed well, but as we know, cars wear out and require upkeep if they are to last. As the miles add up – and if you live in the north like I did – you deal with extremes in climate and temperature, not to mention the salt spread on the road in the winter. All of the above mentioned take their toll on our 'Baby' – our prized classic car.

In our wish to preserve this relic of the past, we painstakingly perform every task needed to keep our 'Baby' looking new. As the motor begins to bellow out blue smoke, we spend hundreds of dollars to rebuild the engine. As the tires and brakes wear out, we replace them. However, as our car's body meets the elements, over time, we need to break out the 'Bondo'[1] and repaint the car's surface. With all the efforts we make to reclaim the original beauty, we manage to keep our 'Baby' looking like a new car.

Through the years, the body and motor wear out, but the basic structure of the frame and undercarriage remains the same. To preserve the car for the next decade, we park our 'Baby' and buy another for everyday use. In an age of change, some items need to be upgraded in order to have better fuel economy, greater speeds, a more stylish look, and better safety equipment.

Similarly, this is how our Native American Christian churches operate. We try over the years to preserve our 'Baby'. In this case, our older traditional-styled church – our relic from the past – is the

---

[1] A brand of automotive body filler.

'Baby'. We try to preserve our Native American churches by rebuilding the engine, (changing pastors), adding Bondo and new paint (adding new programs and new pews), all in an effort to hide our flaws and weaknesses. When in reality, our underlying structure is holding us back from being the vehicle God wants to use to reach our Native communities effectively in these new days. Like well-preserved classic cars, our Native churches must change, update, and transition in order to become effective in the future. To stagnate in ineffective methods of evangelism for long periods of time is unhealthy. If we are to move into the future and surpass the results of our predecessors – which have given us fewer than 5 percent of the Native population claiming to be Christian – change is essential.

Change Happens

The word 'change' means a transition from one state, condition, or phase to another.[2] Whether we want it or not, we all experience change. We will all become older, maybe a little heavier, or our hair will become thin and gray. The world around us is also changing at an ever-increasing pace. Nevertheless, amid all the changes, some of our Native churches are intent on upholding an older status quo in ministry. These ministries have fond memories they refer to as the 'good old days'.

As much as we would prefer to avoid change, it will happen. On the one hand, many view change in our Native churches with uneasiness. Most approach change with a negative attitude – especially when it comes to facing change in our established traditions and habits. On the other hand, other Native churches view change and transition as an exciting experience. How could the same word elicit two such different responses? One reason is the way we approach change and transition. We must not view change as something to be feared but as a friend. My goal in writing about change and transition is to help Native American churches and Native leaders dispel the fear associated with change. Learning about the process of change and transition will give them some 'handles' they can use in order to manage change and transition to create the Native church of the future.

---

[2] *American Heritage Dictionary* (Boston, MA: Houghton Mifflin, 1985), p. 116.

Is This Book for You?

I am writing this book for Native pastors and lay leaders who:

- Are struggling with the Native American Contextual Ministry Movement approach.

- Would like some practical advice in creating positive changes in their traditional-style churches.

- Realize that we cannot continue in our present methods if we want to see the next generation of Native people saved.

- Are uncomfortable with the realization that they will stand before God someday and be asked if they did all they possibly could to make coming to faith as simple as possible.

- Are ready for change.

How to Use This Book

This book is the result of my research on organizational change, barriers to change, and the best approaches to making change. I am writing to introduce ideas and approaches for making change and transition achievable without anxiety. I am specifically writing to encourage those who are ready for change. This book contains personal experiences, specific situations, proven approaches, and practical advice for you to approach change and transition without fear.

God spoke to Joshua and said, 'Have I not commanded you? Be strong and of good courage; do not be afraid, nor be dismayed, for the LORD your God is with you wherever you go' (Josh. 1.9). We need to go into the 'new territory of change' to Contextual Ministry with the same courage.

Why write a book about change and transition?

The purpose of this book is to help pastors and church leaders to develop a better understanding of the transitions and changes we face in order to transition to a Native American Contextual Ministry. Dr. Darrell Whiteman, former Dean of the E. Stanley Jones School of Evangelism at Asbury Theological Seminary in Kentucky, 'caught the vision' for the Contextual Movement. As a result, Asbury seeks to encourage those involved in the Native American Contextual Movement. Dr. Whiteman says of the movement, 'We are in a Kairos time',[3] meaning this is a God moment happening in our midst. 'We need to ask the question, where are you going, God? Then we go where God is going instead of inviting him to go along with our plan', says Samuel Chand in his eye-opening book, *Futuring: Leading Your Church into Tomorrow*.[4] Therefore, if we want to become more effective and fruitful in our ministries, we must take advantage of every opportunity we are given. At this 'Kairos' time, we must do whatever is necessary to help lead our lost Native people to a personal relationship with Jesus Christ. In *How to Change Your Church Without Killing It*, Alan Nelson shares this comment: 'Go for it! Be strong. Dream new dreams. Honor the past, but do not live there. God has too much in store for us in the promised lands he has prepared for our churches.'[5] My hope is that as you read this book you will experience God in a new and powerful way. So, with Nelson's motivating words, let us press on to 'the promised land'.

---

[3] North American Institute for Indigenous Theological Studies Symposium, Crestmont College, Ranchos Verdes, CA, 2004.

[4] Samuel Chand, *Futuring: Leading Your Church into Tomorrow* (Grand Rapids, MI: Baker Books, 2002), p. 139.

[5] Alan Nelson and Gene Appel, *How to Change Your Church Without Killing It* (Grand Rapids, MI: Zondervan, 2000), p. xvii.

INTRODUCTION

Before he ascended to heaven, Jesus told his disciples: 'Go therefore and make disciples of all the nations, baptizing them in the name of the Father and of the Son and of the Holy Spirit, teaching them to observe all things that I have commanded you' (Mt. 28.19-20). The commissioning of Jesus' disciples appears five times in Matthew, Mark, Luke, John, and Acts. God is trying to make something clear to us. But Jesus did not give us specific instructions as to how to go about carrying out the Great Commission. Although spoken to those living in the Jewish community, God did not say we should forever fulfill these marching orders only from a Jewish perspective – or in our situation only from within what I call a 'white north Atlantic male-dominated theological context'. I believe we can fulfill our commission no matter what our context is, whether African, Chinese, South American – or even Native American. I believe God not only gave us our unique languages but also our cultures and the permission to use our various cultural expressions to honor Him (Acts 17.26).

Jesus encourages our efforts by stating, 'I will build my church, and the gates of Hades shall not prevail against it' (Mt. 16.18). As I look at the condition of the churches in Native America, we have not done so well. With over 450 years of evangelism, fewer than 5 percent of the Native population in the United States self-identify as Christian. Not impressive results considering the time, money, and sweat poured into evangelism efforts across the country.[1] With such limited results, it seems to me the gates of Hades have threatened to

---

[1] Richard Twiss, *One Church, Many Tribes: Following Jesus the Way God Made You* (Ventura, CA: Regal Books, 2000), p. 79.

prevail in our Native American ministries. This is not unique only to the Native American churches, as is highlighted by the Barna Research Group:

(1) Churches in the Protestant denominations have lost members while the population has increased.

(2) Many of the churches have not recently added even one new member through conversion.

(3) The younger the adult, the less likely they are to attend a church.

And, if these findings are not enough to show our failure, Barna adds, 'Today many churches remain open simply because the resources are still there to keep the bills paid, even though they have no relevant connection or ministry to the people who appear in their communities'.[2]

With findings like these, we need to take Jesus' Great Commission seriously. He says, 'And surely I am with you always, even to the end of the age' (Mt. 28.20). The use of this phrase, 'to the end of the age', tells me that with every culture everywhere in every age, the Holy Spirit's power will be with us to fulfill the commission. We need to go back to when, where, and how we have failed in reaching Native people.

Change is not an Option

In the mid-nineties, I was a member of an older inner-city church, (Burton Heights United Methodist Church) which, as in the example above, spent most of its income repairing the old building and paying the bills. However, the members of the church longed to make a difference. So, I was asked to attend a Willow Creek Community Church conference in Chicago and bring back a message of hope for this dying church. The message I brought back and shared with them was too big a 'leap' for the members to make. They realized they had to do something – but they did not know how to make the needed changes. They did not understand the process of change and what

---

[2] George Barna, *The Second Coming of the Church* (Nashville, TN: Word, 1999), p. 156.

would be required of them. Confusion and heated discussion over how to continue were the result. Their conclusion was to remain the same and face an uncertain future. To explain why people choose not to change, Dr. Charles Kraft of Fuller Theological Seminary in Pasadena, California says, 'Often people will reject a solution to their problem because they do not believe there could be any solution to it'.[3] Today, Burton Heights United Methodist Church is no longer open. The building quickly sold to another Christian organization that had decided to make whatever changes necessary in order to reach their community.

If we are not good stewards of all that has been placed in our hands, we will end up in similar situations. Change is not an option; it is a necessity if our Native ministries are to thrive.

Change and Transition are Necessary

I grew up in a Bible-believing church in southwest Lower Michigan. The Salem Indian Mission United Methodist Church was the center of our lives. I have fond memories of Sunday School, church camps and revivals, and seasonal holiday services. Our church was traditional Methodist. Our pastor, my uncle Reverend Lewis White Eagle Church, diligently served two churches in the same Native community. Although small in attendance and known as a family church, we worshiped and served God with our whole hearts. I came to faith in this church, and it will always have a special place in my heart. My childhood church had such a strong influence on me. Yours must have had the same impact on you too. Even though I speak of the need for change I still feel the need to help these traditional-style churches make the changes necessary to reach their Native communities for Christ. Unlike some pastors and leaders who strive to hang on to the 'good old days', I feel called to create new approaches and develop new models to fulfill our God-given commission. These traditional-style churches managed to reach you and me, but their style is ineffective in reaching the urban Native American of today's generation. Change and transition are not only useful, but also necessary

---

[3] Charles Kraft, *Anthropology for Christian Witness* (Maryknoll, NY: Orbis Books, 1996), p. 392.

for the future growth of our Native churches. 'Yet the most important institution of all – the church – often continues to operate on insights forged in the late nineteenth and early twentieth centuries.'[4] Many Native churches still cling to programs and styles of ministry they used in the 1950s and 60s. These styles are no longer effective. As Rick Warren, pastor of Saddleback Community Church in California, has said is his seminars, 'When the horse is dead it's time to dismount'.[5] George Barna affirms Warren's statement: 'Evangelism is effective when people do whatever is necessary to reach the unchurched, rather than maintain traditions and accept outdated assumptions for the sake of continuity'.[6]

I now live in Albuquerque, New Mexico, and have made friends with Native individuals and families living in a region full of Native people that need Christ. I know that our past methods are not designed to reach them. These unreached Natives need new approaches and methods sensitive to their needs if they are to take our message seriously. Cultural sensitivity is more than not being what we were forty or eighty years ago – cultural sensitivity celebrates differences and change.[7] Cultural sensitivity and the willingness to change ministry approaches are also means for reaching our children. If we do not do something soon, we will lose them or – as we are finding out – we have already lost many of them. Two of our five children have accepted Christ as a result of our using new styles of evangelism. If you are a believer, as my wife and I are, reaching your family is your first priority. We both know of pastors' families who have spent so much time reaching out to the world that they neglected those in their own homes. We know that neglecting our families is not the biblical model. It does highlight some of the pressures of ministry.

Some of the following stages of change are reflected in the churches in our communities. First is the 'Declining Church'. Many of our Native churches are in decline. Without needed changes and improvement in the way they approach ministry, these churches will stay in decline. Some will manage to maintain for a few more years,

---

4 James White, *Rethinking the Church: A Challenge to Creative Redesign in an Age of Transition* (Grand Rapids, MI: Baker Books, 2003), p. 18.

5 'Purpose Driven Church Conference', Saddleback Community Church, Lake Forest, CA, 1994.

6 Barna, *The Second Coming of the Church*, p. 156.

7 Chand, *Futuring*, p. 78.

but will not be as effective as they could be. Without change, these churches like many others will come to a point when they will consider whether or not to lock their doors. This is a sad fate for many Native churches. They have lost a relevant connection with the people they want to reach.

Another stage of existence is the 'Surviving Church'. Surviving Native churches go about ministry by just keeping the church machine working. Nothing new ever happens in these churches. They minister to those already in their congregations but they lack the vision and strategy to create a church that can effectively reach out to Native people in their communities. It is not that they do not want to be more effective; they just do not know how to go about it or where to begin.

Still another stage is the 'Growing Church'. These churches have found methods that have an edge over the declining and surviving churches. The problem is that their growth is often gained at the expense of other churches. Rick Warren refers to these churches as the 'Hot Churches in town'. They have managed to become popular, so they attract people from stagnant churches because they want more from their worship experience. Many people who move to these churches do so out of selfishness, wanting a church to meet 'their' needs. Warren also says these people see the new 'service' as 'serve us'.[8] Many of these churches care about outreach and they support the mission efforts attached to their churches. Sponsoring missionaries and other parachurch ministry work with Indigenous peoples in other countries, they are unaware that they sit within communities that are a mission field in and of themselves. Growing Native churches grow because other Native Christian people join their churches. Growing churches usually have an awesome music ministry, a dynamic preacher, or a youth ministry that surpasses other smaller congregations.[9]

The fourth stage is the 'Progressive Church'. The progressive churches are needed to reach the thousands of Native people without Christ. They must their work among Native churches with 'Church growth eyes' as Peter Wagner says – not depending on transferring

---

[8] 'Purpose Driven Church Conference', Saddleback Community Church, Lake Forest, CA, 1997.
[9] 'Purpose Driven Church Conference', 1997.

Christian Natives to their fold but intentionally doing whatever it will take to become a friend of change in a complacent church world.[10] These churches seek to become evangelistic, appropriating plans and strategies or developing growing understanding like other churches and using contextual ministry methods. Contextually-minded churches are not new. The Apostle Paul used contextual approaches in the churches he planted. This is one reason his ministries had such dramatic results.

Roland Allen, missionary to China in the 1930s, was a man ahead of his time when he wrote a book entitled, *Missionary Methods: St. Paul's or Ours?*[11] This book has given many of today's pastors and leaders interested in contextual ministry the inspiration to break with traditional methods and start Indigenous churches – churches that look, sound, and act like the people in their communities. A contextual style of service is simply a service in which a context is created that allows seekers to explore Christianity in a way that moves them 'down the line' toward the event of salvation.[12] It is this type of church that we will explore in the balance of this book.

Making it your method

As you review the various stages of Native church development, where does your own church fit? Are you satisfied with your present state? Are Christ's words in the Great Commission compelling you to build effective churches? Is your church able to reach the Native people in your community who need Christ, or are you content to minister to those already persuaded? Are you ready to share the life-changing message of the gospel by meeting Native people where they are spiritually – even those still involved in traditional Native beliefs and practices? Do you need to expand your circle to include those Native people living somewhere between traditional customs and those not attending at all because they are disillusioned with our present church methods? You can adjust the approaches used in your existing churches in order to reach the lost. I suggest that starting

---

[10] C. Peter Wagner, former professor of Church Growth at Fuller Theological Seminary.

[11] Roland Allen, *Missionary Methods: St. Paul's or Ours?* (Grand Rapids, MI: Eerdmans, 1996).

[12] White, *Rethinking the Church*, p. 57.

new contextual ministries is the best way to meet the needs of the growing urban Native population. Today nearly 75 percent of the Native populations live in urban centers. The number of non-believing Natives is growing as it is among other people groups. There are cynics, skeptics, spectators, and seekers within our Native communities. When developing new approaches, we need to create the right atmosphere so Natives in all stages can find Christ. We need different styles of churches to meet all the needs. We do not just want more Native members in our churches; we want people who have a true relationship with Christ. In new contextual churches, the point is not to make them 'Indian' churches, but to use the familiar forms found within traditional Native practices to honor God. Contextual ministry's focus is to tell them about Christ in a culturally-sensitive environment. Pastor Kyle Taylor of White Eagle Ministries in Oklahoma for several years has used an approach called 'Common Ground'. He uses this approach very effectively in reaching the Natives in his region. Pastor Kyle quotes the Living Bible translation, which says, 'Yes, whatever a person is like, I try to find common ground with him so that he will let me tell him about Christ and let Christ save him' (1 Cor. 9.22).[13] Today, Kyle is on staff at Bacone College in Muskogee, Oklahoma as retention specialist.

So where does your church fit into this picture? Does your ministry reflect the approaches used by the European-style of church? Are you ready – or closer than you were before – to start reaching lost Natives with new contextual methods? I know your concerns about the opposition that exists toward those courageous enough to try contextual ministry styles. I know the tension and fear many of you feel in even beginning to think of using contextual ministry methods. I know you, like me, have heard it said (as it has been said for the last 450 years) that our Native ways are wrong. It will be a while before we can accept that our Native ways are neither better nor worse than any other culture. Our cultural expressions can become acceptable expressions of genuine worship to Jesus Christ just as European cultural ways have been. I managed to face my fears when challenged to try another approach after attending Willow Creek Community Church's conference in 1992. The approaches they recommended

---

[13] Pastor Kyle Taylor, White Eagle Ministries, Tulsa, Oklahoma.

took hold in my life and ministry. I adopted and adapted those practices and principles I felt would best work to reach urban Native Chicago residents in more effective ways.

Consider your church's location within the process of adopting
contextual styles. God wants leaders who see the need for change and
draw closer in understanding this new model. He also wants Native
people to recognize that **he created us as Native Americans and
not as white Europeans**. This book is about helping you and your
church consider contextual ministry styles, make the transition, and
feel good about your decision.

Satan has had us locked up in ineffective approaches for far too
long. God wants his people to trust him and to become part of the
solution. God wants us to use our creativity and search for biblical
methods that will better connect with the thousands of seeking Native people outside our church doors. I am encouraged because, over
the past few years, I have seen many Native ministry leaders and Native churches making the necessary changes in order to reach Native
people for Christ. Some churches are starting to make small changes
because of what they have learned at contextual conferences such as
those offered by Wiconi International or the North American Institute for Indigenous Theological Studies (NAIITS). Others are ready
to take a bigger leap and change their style of service to a contextual
model by incorporating a true Christian expression of worship in the
Native style. We do not make these changes because they seem 'neat'
or 'cool'. We make the changes because God is leading us to adopt
new approaches for his glory and the purpose of effectively sharing
the gospel.

1

LET'S FACE THE FACTS AND GET REAL

Although I am proposing change in our Native churches, I must remind you that I came to faith in a traditional church. The Salem Indian Mission United Methodist Church is typical of many Native churches across the country. I have fond memories of my childhood church – perhaps you do as well. If your church history is like mine, an Auntie taught Sunday school, and the pastor was probably also a relative. We had summer vacation Bible school, and an annual revival meeting was preached by a Native evangelist whom we all knew. In just such a church, I committed my life to serve Christ and his Church. *I owe a debt of gratitude to my childhood church, and so do many of you.* Even considering all the fond memories and the good work that came from them, these churches are not effective for this century. I am not putting down these Native churches. I have a passion to see Native people saved and to see new approaches used to evangelize them – either in current churches or in new ministries initiatives. However, more important than starting a new church and supporting the new model is the awareness that God is the initiator in today's contextual ministry movement. Although we came to faith in these Native churches, we know there are thousands of Native people who will never have the same experience or opportunity we had. As I stated earlier, less than 5 percent of Native people across the country claim to be Christian. This statistic must be changed.[1] To

---

[1] Twiss, *One Church*, p. 79.

reach the Native population we will need to adapt and adopt, make some critical decisions, and step forward with courage not fear.

Having had the opportunity to visit many Native churches, I think there is a great need for us to take a closer look at our effectiveness. Most of those attending Native churches are from families who have been there for generations. We need to realize that across-the-board, our Native churches are either on a plateau or are declining in attendance, and we need to face the fact that many of our Native churches are closing their doors. Nelson and Appel comment,

> The sad reality is that in each generation, the American churches [and Native churches] are becoming less effective. If the church is unable to navigate change and communicate the Gospel to a changing world, our grandchildren and great-grandchildren [in our Native communities] may have little chance of attending church, much less coming to faith.[2]

These are not just my thoughts – other Native churches and ministry leaders agree. **Let's get real. Something has to change!**

If your Native-church experience is similar to mine, your church has probably never had traditional Native people (what we might call 'Powwow' Natives) in the congregation. Although raised in a Native community with Christian and traditional Native people, I did not understand why there was such division between these two groups. It became clear that the major problem was the rigid set of rules imposed upon people in order for them to attend our Christian churches. The traditional people are expected to leave their Native identity outside the church doors. One incident stands out in my mind. A well-known traditional family came to Sunday service. Tension filled the air in the church. Members exchanged cordial greetings with them but not the kind extended to those from non-traditional Native families in our community. The atmosphere of the service was not the same as usual. Regular attendees were watching every move of our visitors with a certain coolness. After the church, the visiting family left without so much as a good-bye or 'hope to see you next week' response. We found out later that this family was experi-

---

[2] Nelson and Appel, *How to Change Your Church*, p. 3.

encing problems at home and came to church for some encouragement. Because of deep-seated differences, they left without feeling God's love and grace, only disconnectedness.

Our visitors had to attend our church with all of our European liturgical forms and formal methods – none of which were culturally-sensitive to their Native lifestyle. Then they had to face their Christian neighbors' attitudes. They needed to hear of God's love and grace in a way sensitive to the cultural forms that were familiar to them and not in the way we have come to accept as normal.

This illustration does not mean the ways our Native church worshiped were wrong. It does suggest there is a need to provide an alternative approach so our traditional neighbors can experience Christ in a form more sensitive to who they are. My church's theology was biblical, but its methods and attitudes prevented that family from ever coming back.

If this church scenario sounds familiar, would you be willing to adapt and change so similar families could hear the life-changing message of Jesus? The Apostle Paul said, 'I become all things to all men so that by all possible means I might save some. I do all this for the sake of the gospel' (1 Cor. 9.23). Would you make some changes in your methods for the sake of the gospel?

The Apostle Paul's methods included adapting and adopting to reach those from different backgrounds. My proposed approach may sound liberal to some of you, but in fact, it is St. Paul's method, and God called him his chosen instrument. Churches like Paul's will thrive across the next centuries. Mike Regale says in his book entitled, *Death of the Church*,

> What about the literally thousands of churches across America in which no progressive strategies are attempted? Let us be frank, in reality, many of them will not see the dawn of the twenty-first century. Many more will pass away by the end of the first decade. We have looked at the demographics. There is no future for most. Let us stop the denial!'[3]

Mike Regale's words sound harsh, but they speak the truth.

---

[3] Mike Regale, *Death of the Church* (Grand Rapids, MI: Zondervan, 1995), pp. 184-85.

In this millennium, we face the challenge of communicating the gospel to a generation of Native people far removed from the era we grew up in. When Paul set out to reach the gentiles, he had to use approaches that were different from those used with the Jews. Corinth and Athens resemble our Native American communities today, and our methods will need to be adapted to build a Native bridge to their world. We need to realize the style and techniques we have used in the past will not be highly effective in today's urban Native communities. Unless we adjust, we will do no better than the white missionaries did for generations. *It would be a shame if we ended up losing another generation of Native people because we are too stubborn to make necessary changes.* We need to stay firmly committed to the message found in our traditional churches but be flexible in our methods in order to reach a new generation of urban Native people.

Same Message Different Culture

Throughout history, Christian missionaries have been faced with the challenge of communicating the gospel across language and cultural barriers. We too need to reevaluate how we communicate and connect with a postmodern Native world through Native 'cultural language'. We know that more effective methods could have been used to reach Natives in the past, but they were not. In some cases, the mind-set of earlier missionaries became rigid. In attempting to reach the new urban Natives, I have drastically changed my approach. Native people today do not have the basic scriptural knowledge we were privileged to grow up with. What is constant though is the need to find meaning and purpose in life. As a result, our teaching must begin with what most of us might view as a 'Sunday school class'. We should begin with stories and themes we consider well-known, realizing that most of these new Native seekers do not know them. To them they are new stories. There are countless ways this can be achieved, but the key is to begin where people are and then to make the message as clear and compelling as possible.[4] We ought to present the same message to different cultures in several different ways – realizing different times call for different actions.

---

[4] Barna, *The Second Coming*, p. 40.

In the business world, much thinking goes into understanding the customer. Marketers search for what the customer wants in an ever-changing marketplace. Their bottom line is sales; our bottom line is new believers. We need to present the 'unchanging message of the gospel' to our 'customers' in the values and vernacular of the un-saved. We must adjust our methods to their needs and begin thinking like missionaries in a foreign mission field. We need to learn as much as we can about the urban Native person. As Rick Warren says, 'We need to put the hook right in front of their faces'[5] to catch them. Insights and processes that once brought success now guarantee failure. The old way of business simply will not work anymore.[6]

Can we foresee a new Native American church that loves the lost and tries to fulfill the Great Commission in new and creative ways? Is the church willing to consider change in order to present the un-changing message of the gospel, thus building a bridge to this new unreached people group? As Native missionaries to our own people, we must earn their trust and respect as Native pastors, something early foreign missionaries were unable to do. This compelling love for the lost will make adapting and adopting change an easy process. When proposing the adoption of change, we always need to remind the Church that, **'It's not about you, it's about them'.** What I mean is we have Christ, they do not, and we must be willing to do as Paul said, 'become all things to all men' so that some might be saved (1 Cor. 9.23).[7]

Think Outside the Box

Many of us have used the same methods and practices week after week and year after year in our churches and never questioned our actions. What we fail to see in the biblical stories is that the God we serve has repeatedly used new methods throughout history. The scriptures are teeming with his words to do something new. Here are just a few of my favorite verses where God speaks about 'change':

---

[5] 'Purpose Driven Church Conference', 1997.
[6] White, *Rethinking the Church*, p. 18.
[7] 'Purpose Driven Church Conference', 1997.

- I will give them an undivided heart and put a new spirit in them; I will remove from them their hearts of stone and give them a heart of flesh (Ezek. 11.19).

- Forget the former things; do not dwell on the past. See I am doing a new thing! Now it springs up, do you not perceive it? I am making a way in the desert and streams in the wasteland (Isa. 43.18-19).

- Neither do men pour new wine into old wineskins. If they do, the skins will burst, the wine will run out and the wineskins will be ruined. No, they pour new wine into new wineskins and both are preserved (Mt. 9.17).

- Now, by dying to what once bound us, we have been released from the law so that we serve in a new way of the Spirit and not in the old way of the written code (Rom. 7.6).

- Therefore, if anyone is in Christ, he is a new creation; the old has gone, the new has come! (2 Cor. 5.17).

The Jewish religious leaders thought they had God all figured out, and they lorded it over the people. In that way they showed their devotion. However, Jesus had another plan and wanted them, as the scriptures show, to see he had change in mind. Scripture reveals to us that God comes into our lives and introduces change. God refuses to be put in a box of man-made rules and traditions. The rules and traditions created by religious leaders seem even more prone than others to become traditions that are believed to be close to infallible, notes Charles Kraft.[8] God wants to do new things through his people and is frustrated by our stubbornness and our resistance to change. God has always done new things and even old things in new ways. My point is that change is good and sometimes necessary. Nevertheless, we view 'new' as different, and we try to resist. We face the new with, 'We've never done it that way before'. In his book entitled, *Diffusion of Innovation*, Everett Rogers makes us aware that new ideas and methods start out with resistance and gradually become accepted over time.[9]

---

[8] Kraft, *Anthropology for Christian Witness*, p. 380.
[9] Everett Rogers, *The Diffusion of Innovation* (New York, NY: The Free Press, 4th edn, 1995), p. 392.

As human beings, we seek the familiar because it is safe. But God is in control, and he knows what is best for us. We disobey when we refuse to see just how big he can be. My goal with this book is to help us see the desire of God's heart and to trust him as we go through change and transition. So, be encouraged when you lead your people in new directions!

2

MOTIVATION FOR CHANGE

Before diving right into some of the technical information dealing with organizational change, I would like to share some of my personal reasons for pursuing change. The deep changes that have occurred in my life have mostly resulted from spiritual events. I received my call to ministry in 1988. I thought I would follow my uncle's example and serve in my home church after attending a Bible college. As my calling began to come into a sharper focus, I received further guidance from God in 1992 through a vision/dream. Through God's inspiration, I followed a path of ministry unlike the one I had imagined. I began to see mission to Native Americans as my calling, and I grew ever more critical of our present methods. When I first heard of the low statistical numbers of Natives who claim to be Christian, my heart broke. I then decided that if I were going to minister to Native people, I would do whatever was necessary to increase the percentage of new Christian Natives. This motivation led me to study previous efforts used to evangelize our Native people. As I reviewed the history of Native missions, I was shocked to learn that we as Native ministers have repeated the same ineffective methods used mostly by white missionaries for years. It was clear that their methods needed to be reexamined, especially those that attempted to take away our people's cultural identity.

God made me a Native American and not a white European. God will be honored when we use aspects of our Native culture to worship him, just as white north Atlantic Europeans did in the past when they created true Christian expression of worship from their own cultural beliefs. Implementing these changes is part of God's plan for my life along with others who are like-minded. With God's guidance we have set in motion a method called 'Contextual Native American Ministry'.

This inspiration was all the motivation that my heart needed to create in me a desire to make the biggest possible impact for the Kingdom of God with the remainder of my life. I looked back on the poor results after 450 years of mission to Native Americans and knew that because of the lack of innovation and change, hundreds of thousands of Native people died without Christ. I plan to do my part to introduce the innovation and change it will take to have hundreds of thousands of Native people passing from this world having accepted Jesus as their savior.

What is Your Motivation for Change?

My motivation for change inspires me to identify which methods need to change, and the rest of my ministry deals with how to make those needed changes. We must know up front that not all approaches to Native Ministry should be abandoned, but many of those methods we keep must be reinvented. We cannot approach Native ministry thinking, 'all is well' when the results say otherwise. Bill Hybels tells of a sailboat race he and his crew entered. During their practice, they did quite well, but when they tried to perform some basic maneuvers, they failed terribly. When their practice was over, Hybels sat down with his crew and walked carefully through the basic techniques for a sailing team. The basic techniques are critical in both sailing and ministry.[1] In his book entitled, *Courageous Leadership*, Hybels relates advice he received from his friend Peter Drucker. Drucker asks the questions: 'Why are we in business?' And additionally, 'Who is our customer?'[2] Likewise, we need to evaluate our ministries by asking ourselves, 'Why do we exist and what are we trying to achieve?'

How do these two questions fit your ministry? It might just be me, but I see the existence of some of our Native churches as an 'end' in

---

[1] Bill Hybels, 'WCC Church Growth Seminar', Willow Creek Community Church, South Barrington, IL, 1992.

[2] Bill Hybels, *Courageous Leadership* (Grand Rapids, MI: Zondervan, 2001), p. 53.

and of themselves. I believe that deep in their hearts they want all Native people to repent and accept Christ. Christ desires to have all come to faith. Some churches, because of a lack of leadership and a compelling vision, exist in a complacent world far removed from an evangelism that requires risk and sacrifice. Some have become self-centered and narrow, seeing only their own needs as primary, rather than modeling sacrificial ministry, which stretches their people. We attend our churches knowing the way we do ministry is not going to draw in today's Native people. This is one reason church members do not invite our Native American neighbors. We have lost – if we ever had it at all – the overwhelming need to find common ground (Acts 22.19) with our Native neighbors so we can tell them about Christ. We spend our Sunday mornings and Sunday evenings and Wednesday evening praying services huddled together when thousands remain untouched by our lives and God's message. We have heard sermon after sermon and gained spiritual weight when we should be exercising our faith by reaching out to those who are in need of a savior.

I realize that I come down a little hard on ineffective patterns and church practices, but this section is about motivation, and we need to look at ours again. The balance of this section will lead us in growing in our motivation as leaders and increasing our evangelistic ministry vision.

Where do we begin? We need to start by reevaluating our church's mission. Our mission statements, in some cases, have become only print on pages. They need to become our motivation to action. We become very attached to our methods over time. They become less and less effective yet ever more important to us. Christ's Great Commission should be our sacred marching order. But we make our methods sacred and end up fighting for and defending our methods as higher priorities than the commission. The high value we place on the lost is what should drive us. The commission says, 'Go into the entire world and preach the gospel, making disciples, teaching them to observe all things' (Mt. 28.19-20). However, some portray the commission as I restate it here, 'Stay within the safe walls of your church, and preach the gospel to only those who attend, making sure they are excessively discipled by teaching them to obey all things, but not to those who need it'.

We have lost the relevant and effective touch we had in the past. We were relevant and effective thirty or forty years ago and some believe what worked back then is suitable for today as well. 'Past success has blinded them to the importance of seeing the implications of the changing world and to admit that past accomplishments will not guarantee future success.'[3] ***To overcome our clinging to the past we need to spell faith as – RISK and risk involves the way we do ministry.*** James says, 'Faith without works is dead' (Jas 2.26). Therefore, faith with works is alive. This living faith needs to be reflected in the way we do our Heavenly Father's business. The values we place on our programs and budget should show our faith at work. As a result, your ministry will become relevant and effective once again.

Being relevant means: 'Relating to the matter at hand, to the point, applicable to current issues, distinctive'.[4] Does this characterize your church's mission? Relevant for today's Native church means understanding how new ideas and ministry concepts can be implemented to fit our outreach. Their lack of relevance is causing us to grow further from a mission mind-set and is making the unbelieving Native more distant and harder to reach. The church we grew up in will not ever be as effective as it once was, so we have to seek out, with God's help, new ministry approaches for our churches.

I believe implementing culturally-relevant approaches to reach Native people is the cure for our inertia. God is not honored by our refusal to seek out other avenues to achieve the same goal. Your present style of ministry is precious to you and your congregation, but people without Christ are a precious and much higher priority in God's sight. We must come to the realization that a method of evangelism that once worked is not the only system for today, just as various methods used by Europeans are no longer used today. This will mean that our older methods will have to go and new ones must be incorporated in their place.

If you truly believe God's will for your church is to continue using ineffective methods to reach the lost, then stand firm in your convictions. If not, then you must seriously listen to what God is saying. If your church is content to serve the already-Christian Native, then all

---

3 White, *Rethinking the Church*, p. 25.
4 *American Heritage Dictionary*, p. 581.

you may need to do is repackage the same program repeatedly to create an illusion of change. However, those who have seen a glimpse of what God can do are ready to face whatever changes are necessary. Jesus put it this way, 'I have come down from heaven not to do my will but to do the will of him who sent me' (Jn 6.38). It is hard to believe that those who are unwilling to change are saying their preferred style of ministry – even if irrelevant or ineffective – is God's will. They should be reminded that they would be held accountable to God for their unwillingness to follow God's direction – even if that means change.

Styles of music, worship, and preaching follow cultural preferences. Rick Warren says,

> The Bible tells us to meet regularly, but does not tell us when and how often, to teach but not how to organize classes, to take an offering but not how to spend it, and other such instructions without 'specific' procedures to carry them out. God did this on purpose so each church in every culture could create its own unique expression. What we do is establish preferences, which become traditions we feel are the most biblical models to use. Then when our preferences are challenged, we would rather break fellowship or have a church split than change. It is easier to change our theology than to change our order of worship.[5]

These and other preferences are presented to Natives as biblical truth, as requirements for valid church practice, and occasionally even for our salvation. Let us remember the Jerusalem council that debated whether gentiles should be required to keep the Law of Moses in order to be saved (Acts 15). The early Christians, like us today, had a hard time understanding what God is able to do. Therefore, when we see new movements of the Spirit in our land, we, like the Jewish believers in Paul's time, have to debate whether God is in the new Contextual Movement or not.

If you study the beginning of European Christianity, you will realize Europe was a pagan world, and over a period of time their cultural forms and preferences became unshakable traditions that were taught to Indigenous people all over the world. If you would like to investigate the pagan roots of our Christian practices more in depth,

---

[5] 'Purpose Driven Church Conference', 1997.

I would suggest reading George Barna and Frank Viola's book, *Pagan Christianity? Exploring the Roots of our Church Practices.*[6] The following verse helped me understand this concept better:

> Why do you look at the speck of sawdust in your brother's eye and pay no attention to the plank in your own eye? How can you say to your brother, brother, let me take the speck out of your eye, when you yourself fail to see the plank in your own eye? You hypocrite, first take the plank out of your eye, and then you will see clearly to remove the speck from your brother's eye (Lk. 6.41).

I use this verse when pointing out the usability of Native culture forms as valid Christian expression. White European missionaries looked at our cultures and believed that our ways were pagan and could not be used to honor God. However, these same missionaries used preferences and traditions that were developed from centuries-old European pagan rituals. What this means to me is that a pagan form can be redeemed, adapted, and adopted as authentic Christian practice. In like manner, we have the white European culture with a plank in its eye, pointing out the speck in the Native culture's eye.

We know there is good and evil in every culture. The challenge is to discover what is suitable for honoring God and what is not. White Christianity has already determined – from their own evaluation – what can be redeemed from their culture for genuine Christian expression. In using Native cultural forms, we must use the same Holy Spirit-guided discernment. Within the remainder of this book, we will approach some of these questions as we continue to understand change and transition.

What's Involved in Transition and Change?

Before we move into understanding change and transition further, here is a brief story from a church where I was once a member. Change and transition had eluded them for decades. More than forty years ago, an uncle of mine married a beautiful Navajo woman and found himself serving God in the southwest until his death. My mother now had her brother living in New Mexico. She would visit

---

6 George Barna and Frank Viola, *Pagan Christianity? Exploring the Roots of our Church Practices* (Carol Stream, IL: Tyndale Momentum, 2008).

every few years to keep in touch and provide encouragement and support. During our years of traveling to the 'land of enchantment' we visited a Native American church in urban Albuquerque. This Native church, like many others in the southwest, was a 'constant' in a world of fast-paced change. For over forty years my mother would travel to Ramah, New Mexico, and along the way we would stop and worship with this solidly unchanged 'lighthouse' in the heart of Albuquerque. Their beautiful little Native American congregation has, from my observation, managed to uphold the high standards of the Native church with all of its 1950's glory. This church, except for the aging membership and small improvements in their church building and parsonage, is for me like stepping back in time. During our visits to this church we met the same people year after year. Throughout the years, different pastors replaced each other in the pulpit. The old pews were replaced with hand-me-down pews donated by larger churches in the area, and those were replaced with individual cushioned chairs but still set in row arrangements. The kitchen has under gone a face lift. The size of the Sunday service remains the same with minor fluctuations. This bastion of stability with its well-established habits and traditions has managed to remain a relic of the past as the world around them has grown rapidly. This small church reminds me of the Amish of the Midwest. Like the Amish, this church and other churches 'have accepted change reluctantly. Often, they seem to protect certain portions of their culture, while gladly changing others', comments Dr. Kraft.[7] These churches have managed to make physical improvements without changing their core values or methods. There are Native churches like this in many cities and rural areas across the United States. It is this type of church and its leadership I am asking to consider change. Those who are willing to 'be bold and courageous' may find the following pages useful.

The above illustration is meant to help us face the facts and 'examine our hearts'. Traditions and habits are fine, but they are not acceptable when they stifle growth with ineffective practices. I believe that transition is much harder for Native churches than other types of organizations. Nelson and Appel make several observations as to why some churches change more slowly. They say churches like this are the 'tradition keepers', charged with preserving the past at all cost.

---

[7] Kraft, *Anthropology*, p. 364.

When churches face change, they step into an area of heightened emotions. Emotion can become a significant hindrance to the success of the change process. Hurt feelings and damaged relationships can happen and avoidance of the issues results. Because the church is not a business, we have a hard time measuring effectiveness until a church faces closure. This forces the consideration of matters of change. These churches and others like them become places where people can escape the massive changes and turmoil they face in the work world and come to church to escape.[8]

Lastly, old-paradigm pastors are usually managers of these tradition-keeper churches, and for change and transition to take place, change leaders are necessary. Barna found that only 5 percent of pastors identify leadership as part of their gift mix.[9] Church managers are many, but leaders needed to influence change are few. 'When pastors who are not wired to think and to behave as leaders supervise congregations, they foster status-quo [which I have heard is Greek for the mess we're in] ministries of incremental changes, which rarely are sufficient for transformation.'[10] There are several reasons for slow change and transition. But I would like to be optimistic if we are to negotiate the changes needed to create effective evangelism approaches. Robert Quinn in his book, *Deep Change* says,

> Most of us seek quantum leaps in our performance level by pursuing a strategy of incremental investment. This strategy simply does not work. The land of excellence is safely guarded from unworthy intruders. At the gates stand two fearsome sentries – risk and learning. The keys to entry are faith and courage.[11]

Quinn's observations are right on. Risk and learning are qualities we must have if we are to make positive changes.

Nelson and Appel believe we can make the needed changes. In their research, they share first a very important positive feature, which is the recognition that our churches have the Holy Spirit. They add that by recognizing our divine guidance, we can move out of our comfort zones.[12] If Native faith communities can trust and believe

---

8 Nelson and Appel, *How to Change Your Church*, p. 44.
9 Barna, *The Second Coming*, p. 36.
10 Nelson and Appel, *How to Change Your Church*, p. 44.
11 Robert Quinn, *Deep Change* (San Francisco, CA: Jossey-Bass, 1996), p. 165.
12 Nelson and Appel, *How to Change Your Church*, p. 44.

that God is behind the Native Contextual Movement, they can suc-
ceed. Second, how we steward our church resources as we catch the
vision will make funding change and transition possible.[13] Third,
since most of our Native churches are family churches with 'opinion
leaders', when those opinion leaders are won over, they will help their
people endure most any discomfort to make change happen.[14] Warren believes that by being so relational, these family churches are al-
most indestructible.[15] Fourth, when we review our church history we
realize that remaining in the status quo is harmful to our faith in God.
God has moved people through change before, and we find that we
grow our best when God leads us into new territories. Most churches
have, in their past, crossed rivers and accomplished significant break-
throughs. Fifth, as Native churches, we have a higher calling to help
people develop a relationship with God. The power of our calling
and our passion to fulfill the Great Commission can make us open
to change. Sixth, under inspired leaders, our churches can be motivated to do most anything. A vision-casting leader can motivate, but
sometimes it is our policy-laden bureaucratic organizations that
thwart flexibility.[16]

Cycle of Life

Native Americans recognize the cycle of life that is reflected in seasonal changes: spring, summer, fall, and winter. They see the human
cycle of life as conception, birth, childhood, young adult, elder, and
death. Aubrey Malphurs, in his book entitled *Strategy 2000*, says the
church also has a life cycle. The following chart shows this life cycle:

---

[13] Nelson and Appel, *How to Change Your Church*, p. 44.
[14] Nelson and Appel, *How to Change Your Church*, p. 44.
[15] 'Purpose Driven Church Conference', 1997.
[16] Nelson and Appel, *How to Change Your Church*, p. 44.

Plateau

Growth   Decline

Birth   Death

Figure 1: Church Life Cycle[17]

This chart illustrates to those opposed to change and transition that change and transition are continually happening in our Native churches whether we like it or not. Some churches start, grow, plateau, enter decline, then die.

We all know churches that have died and closed their doors. The good news is that in our midst there are new Native churches starting. When we realize that change and transition are realities in a church's life, we can see how God is able to raise up new churches using a new ministry paradigm. One such new 'start' happened in Albuquerque. The United Methodist Church there committed to have an operating Native ministry in the city limits and has appointed an ordained minister to undertake the challenge in an established church.

On the one hand, since this book was first written, this United Methodist church-plant in Albuquerque failed after three years and the ordained minister assigned to the task was reassigned to another Native ministry area. On the other hand, our initiative and new model in church planting has thrived well in Albuquerque in the form of a Native-style church service: Soaring Eagle Ministries at Mesa View United Methodist Church. Our mission was to create awareness of the Native Contextual Ministry Movement and show to the new church starts (wherever they are in our cycle of life) how the movement can be successful within their churches. Our attempt to start a contextual church service did very well. We ran our ministry for three years, during which time we were interviewed for several newspaper articles, local Christian television, and the 700 Club where we were awarded 'America's Church of the Week Award'. We were on top of the world emotionally and ready to expand our efforts. Although this new initiative had much promise, we could not anticipate our nation's economic challenges. Times changed for us when in the summer of

---

[17] Aubrey Malphurs, *Pouring New Wine into Old Wineskins: How to Change a Church Without Destroying It* (Grand Rapids, MI: Baker Books, 1997), p. 20.

2007 the economy in the country took a plunge. As a result of my loss of employment as a carpenter, Soaring Eagle Ministries stopped meeting. It was not long after my employment ended that the funding for Lora's program at the University of New Mexico also came to an end. Because we ran this ministry on a volunteer basis, Lora and I could no longer take the time to hold our gathering. During these turbulent times, we focused on maintaining our family life. In many ministry settings, there is a cycle that churches and ministries go through in which times of transition and change happen as a natural course. Our ministry went through some of these changes naturally and others unnaturally, but God was still glorified, and he opened new doors for us.

Everett Rogers also discusses life-cycle patterns in his research. He talks about the life-cycle continuum from 'birth' to 'plateau'. Rogers illustrates the pattern most groups will follow in order to have a well-integrated transition. He makes the following observations, which I have adapted to our situation in contextual ministry. It is my perception that Native pastors and lay leaders would do well to follow these steps in order to facilitate change. Rogers' pattern takes us through these steps:

1. **Knowledge** occurs when Native church leaders/pastors risk exposure to contextual ministry and learn as much as they can about it. They then gain understanding on how it can be worked out in today's Native-ministry world.

2. **Persuasion** occurs when Native church leaders and pastors form favorable attitudes toward contextual ministry.

3. **Decision** occurs when Native church leaders and pastors start at some stage to become actively involved in adapting and adopting contextual ministry approaches.

4. **Implementation** occurs when Native church leaders and pastors put contextual ministry approaches into practice.

5. **Confirmation** occurs when Native church leaders and pastors begin to see the benefits of contextual ministry methods.

Their postive stance toward methodological change is then affirmed.[18]

As we look at these old and new paradigms of ministry, let us examine what needs to happen. I am not suggesting that we stop the old model of church practice altogether. The old model will have its place in ministry as long as there are old-model churches with attendees in need of a pastor and traditional ministry. The new changes suggested here will take place in Native ministries over time. My concern is how we reach the thousands of Native Americans outside the old-paradigm church walls? It is my recommendation that we, as much as possible, work with those Native churches willing to become contextual.

Having worked in the construction trade, I am well-aware that it is harder to remodel than it is to build a new house. Therefore, I stress the need to start new contextual churches in areas of high receptivity. We can do this as was done in Grand Rapids when we intentionally started a contextual church for the Native American people. We called our intentional effort, 'All Tribes Gathering', and we designed the ministry to be contextual in church structure, organization, and style from the first day we began.

When we understand the life cycle of our Native churches, we can use Rogers' model to our benefit. Thus, whether we are at the stage of 'growth' or at a 'plateau' in our life cycle we must continue to be innovative in order to stay vibrant and relevant instead of cycling toward decline.[19]

---

[18] Rogers, *The Diffusion of Innovation*, pp. 162-80.
[19] Rogers, *The Diffusion of Innovation*, p. 17.

3

A CHANGE MODEL

Starting down the path toward change is a smart thing to do. Like many of you, I became satisfied with the status quo in my church. Church had become so routine and predictable that I often wondered what the point of going to church was. It was not until I studied growing churches that I took an interest in understanding the need for change. Nelson and Appel say, 'When we are unaware of change anatomy, we are apt to rebuke people, ideas, and barriers, and view them as enemies instead of processes that can make us healthy and stronger'.[1] You may be surprised to know that many people, denominational leaders, and parachurch organizations (both Native and non-native) strongly oppose the Contextual Movement. These people do not worry me because I realize that throughout church history, whenever there has been a move of God, opposition from religious leaders has followed. The book of Acts tells the story of God doing his best work through methods not accepted by the religious leaders of the day. The Acts 15 account of the Jerusalem council, where Jewish Christians wanted gentile converts first to become Jewish, shows how religious leaders can strongly oppose God's new way of grace.

The following is a primer for those unfamiliar with the process of change. I want to help you bypass the fears surrounding this process. The change process is a well-studied area. I will share with you from Aubrey Malphurs' book entitled, *Pouring New Wine into Old Wineskins: How to Change a Church Without Destroying It*. I will discuss enough of

---

[1] Nelson and Appel, *How to Change Your Church*, p. 53.

the subject to grab your attention in the hope you will pursue further study. Barna reminds us, 'Change is a natural and unstoppable process in every culture; it is a constant process of renewal and development, especially in our Christian church culture'.[2]

However, in order to have renewal and development in our churches, our first step must be understanding the change process using the following eight proposed methods described by Malphurs.[3]

1. Establish a sense of Urgency

When we speak of urgency, we are talking at an emotional level. John Kotter of the Harvard Business School in his book, *Leading Change*, says 'If change is not considered necessary, people will find a thousand ingenious ways to withhold cooperation'.[4] As you might sense from my introduction, I live out this urgency in my ministry. When I speak to groups, they are shocked with my passion for the need to change. As leaders, we must create in our people this same urgency. Romans 12.2 says, 'We are transformed through the renewing of our mind'. We must allow Holy Spirit to change us. We are talking about the lives of Native American people. If lost people matter to God, they should matter to us.[5] We must effectively communicate God's compelling desire to see lost people found. Leaders and pastors need to realize that we will stand before God someday and be asked, 'Did you do all that you could?' I for one, want to answer, 'Yes, I did all I could to make coming to faith for unreached Native people a doable task'. It would be a tragedy if needed change did not happen in our ministries because of our unwillingness to change.

2. Develop and Cast a Compelling Vision

'Casting a vision' is so important to some fast-growing churches that they have incorporated 'casting the same vision' in a different way with a different method every month.[6] Most of us think that if we

---

    [2] Barna, *The Second Coming*, p. 20.

    [3] Malphurs, *Pouring New Wine*, pp. 130-35.

    [4] John Kotter, *Leading Change* (Boston, MA: Harvard Business School Press, 1996), p. 36.

    [5] 'WCC Church Growth Seminar', 1992.

    [6] 'Purpose Driven Church Conference', 1997.

cast a vision for a new ministry one time our people will get it. To you who think like this, I say 'Wake Up'. People in the pew do not get it the first time or even the second. 'The greatest problem of communication is the illusion that it has been accomplished', comments James White in his section entitled, 'Rethinking Evangelism'.[7] The bottom line is that we need to cast the vision repeatedly – again and again.

In contextual ministry, you can cast the vision yourself, but I recommend you let your people hear similar 'visions' from those with other points of view as well. We have talented speakers in our midst who are willing to share their compelling visions for contextual ministry. When you can work together with others to cast the vision as well, you will hear the passion of God's heart more clearly each time. I further encourage you and your key leaders to attend events where you can hear contextual speakers. This is the best way to inspire motivation. Some important questions to ask are: 'Where is your church going?', and 'What will it look like five or ten years from now?'

Early explorers in America found Indigenous people who knew the land and were able to help guide them. Similarly, we need to learn from contemporary Indigenous leaders who have walked the trails of contextual ministry and have seen a glimpse of the future and what it can look like. Because of fear, some pastors and lay people have turned away from such leaders. When we see the pathetic results of our past evangelism efforts, we will begin trusting these forerunners because they are acutely aware that God is about to accomplish something enormous. Like me, you will want to be a part of what God is doing. Their vision of future ministry may be challenging, but it casts a picture of what the Native American churches of tomorrow will look like. Malphurs writes:

> As the paradigm for the church prior to the 1950s continues to self-destruct and collapse, God is raising up a new paradigm of ministry as we approach the third millennium. Not only will churches minister in new and refreshing ways, but so will their pastors.[8]

---

[7] White, *Rethinking the Church*, p. 44.
[8] Malphurs, *Pouring New Wine*, p. 133.

The disastrous situation we are in is similar to Nehemiah's challenge to rebuild the walls of Jerusalem. Like Nehemiah, who could not tolerate the status quo, neither will you. He called attention to the dire situation with these words of vision, 'Come let us rebuild the walls of Jerusalem, and we will no longer be in disgrace' (Neh. 2.17). Similarly, we can rebuild the 'walls' of our Native Churches by understanding and catching the vision for change and transition toward contextual ministry.

3. Frozen Status quo

'Frozen status quo' is a phrase that describes the safe environment for manager-pastors. Manager-pastors are not expected to create change, nor imagine a world where complacent ministries face challenges. Manager-pastors shepherd their flocks toward the safe pastures of sameness. For our change process to flourish it is up to the change-agent pastor or change-agent lay leader of a church to turn up the thermostat and allow a softening to occur. Needed discontent with the 'Frozen status quo' creates an opening for change to enter. Lyle Schaller says, 'It is the job of the change agent to rub raw the sores of discontent'.[9] My experience as a change agent is that it does not help me make many friends. Change agents say what needs to be said, just as the prophets of old did, and their messages were not popular. We realize that through God's eyes, the message he has put in our hearts must be spoken. To voice an unpopular message hurts. But as I tell every group I speak with about change, 'It's not about us; it's about them', meaning it is about the lost Native people who need a savior.

4. Thawing out the Status quo

Thawing out the 'Frozen Status quo' starts by creating dissatisfaction with our present condition and pointing out the results of refusal to change. This is the change agent's job. Dissatisfaction with the way things are can provide a powerful impetus toward change and a desire to improve one's situation in life.[10] Most average church attendees are

---

[9] Lyle Schaller, *The Change Agent* (Nashville, TN: Abingdon Press, 1972), p. 129.
[10] Kraft, *Anthropology*, p. 391.

not aware of the need for change. Therefore, it is our job to tell them. Another way to create discontent is to warn of impending crisis by painting a candid picture of the future of the church if it does not change.

To start the 'thaw', we ask the needed questions about the church's life cycle. No one wants to die as a church, so we need to capitalize on this motivation in order to help Native congregations plan and carry out the change process. Another way (that has worked in my circumstances) to thaw the 'Status quo' is to present change and innovation as opportunities rather than potential threats. As pastors and lay leaders you need to present the advantages of change and the benefits for your church.

5. Create a Plan

Unlike many Sunday sermons, which are long on showing us our problems and short on remedy, we need to propose new models for the future. The change agent must provide preliminary plans for implementation of change in order to give our new methods a foothold. Then further change can come more easily. From my conversations with Native pastors, I have learned that some are aware of the need for change. It is just that they lack the 'how tos' of the implementation of alternative approaches. The 'how tos' touch on each church's mission statement with respect to their program, church building, and worship style. We must look at how we 'do church' as it relates to who we are serving – the already convinced or the lost. The methods we create will be examples for other 'Status quo' churches to model in their efforts to embrace change.

6. Recruit a Team

The best way to help your Native church create an atmosphere of change that is geared to working with non-contextual churches is to invest in taking your opinion leaders and key lay people to seminars such as those at Willow Creek Community Church in South Barrington, Illinois and Saddleback Community Church in Lake Forest, California. This can often be done through satellite simulcast in most major cities. By taking your team to these church seminars, you will be miles ahead of the pack toward becoming a model of a church focused on reaching the lost.

One of the best ways to prepare your church for the transition to a contextual model would be to take your leaders and key lay people to the Wiconi Family Camp held each year in late July in Turner, Oregon. This camp is a living laboratory where leading contextual minsters provide guidance on how to live out a contextual ministry approach. I would also recommend that leaders and lay people follow my schedule on the Wiconi web site, where I present topics on contextual ministry through the year. Further, I would have interested people attend the North American Institute for Indigenous Studies, where all topics of contextual ministry are presented in an academic symposium held at various locations across the USA and Canada. Finally, I recommend the Immersion Class offered by a joint effort of Wiconi International and Sioux Falls Seminary, where individual and groups can learn both the theological basis of contextual ministry and the practical methods for implementing such a ministry. By attending these events, your church leaders will come to understand the needs of Native churches and find ways to adapt contextual ministry innovations to your circumstances.

I had such a team at our church start in Grand Rapids in the mid-1990s. Our team had attended megachurch seminars, which made starting our contextual church that much easier. They also had the benefit of my extensive experience in contextual ministry as we trained a small group in the methods and approaches of contextual ministry. As a result, our group understood the above paradigms and we started our contextual church with a team that only God could have assembled. Not all Native churches will be as prepared as we were; but with persistence, they can create in their membership the motivation to journey toward needed change by taking risks and learning all they can through the resources are available today.

7. Implementation

Once you have done all you can to educate your team and expose them to growing churches and contextual models, you will be ready to carry out change in your own church. There are those of us who are eager to help you move through the steps to incorporate new models of change. Call on those who have weathered the storms to set a course to work toward Native worship styles and to help develop contextual methods that can work for you and your unique group. You will be well on your way to adapting and adopting the Native expressions of worship best suited to your area. The benefit of starting new contextual ministries such as our 'All Tribes Gathering' is as Kraft comments, 'From the point of view of the communicator, the key concept is "demonstration." If the usefulness of something can be demonstrated, it is very likely to be accepted.'[11]

8. Refreeze

Having stepped forward into the incorporation of various worship methods from our Native traditions, you can now 'Refreeze', but be careful to use only those expressions of worship you have studied and prayed over and feel comfortable using. Our ministries in Grand Rapids and Albuquerque created a model of contextual ministry that might be far beyond your comfort zone. We are striving to break new ground and lead the way so you can see and feel a functioning contextual church/ministry that exemplifies what I like to call 'Authentic Christianity from a Native American Point of View'. At this point, you 'Refreeze', but you need to leave room for another round of these same steps.

---

[11] Kraft, *Anthropology*, p. 394.

4

TRANSITIONING

Progressing from a 'Frozen Status Quo' to 'Refreeze', to the 'New Status Quo' involves transition. William Bridges notes in his book, *Managing Transition*, 'Unless transition occurs, change will not work'.[1] I am well-aware of the need for successful transition in both method and leadership. In 2000, my wife and I made plans to move from Grand Rapids, Michigan to Albuquerque, New Mexico. Our contextual church, 'All Tribes Gathering', was running smoothly at the time. I had been preparing our team for the change they were about to face. We chose a successor for the church and felt good about the choice. Although our new pastor had been with us from the start, he had not fully understood what would be required of a pastor leading a church in this unique style of ministry. All Tribes Gathering stayed active for several years, and then the gathering acquired a leader who would endeavor to take it to a new level and in a new direction. Mike Peters caught the contextual vision and took on those members of All Tribes Gathering wanting to continue to worship in an authentic Native Christian expression, calling it 4 Fires. He also started an extension church in northern Michigan and has become a valuable promoter of the need for contextual methods and approaches in ministry. 4 Fires has been blessed by God and is moving in exciting directions under his capable leadership.

The transition process you will face when adopting contextual methods will be similar to our pastoral leadership transition process.

---

[1] William Bridges, *Managing Transition* (Reading, MA: Perseus Books, 1991), p. 3.

It is important to follow God's leading. You must have deep conviction in order to maintain the necessary momentum required to become an established contextual church/ministry. Your capacity to keep the motivation high and deal with emotional obstacles will determine your success. Bridges shows how he views transition as Ending – Neutral Zone – Beginning.

Transition starts with an ending and ends with a beginning. The middle is where we face our fears. We would rather be solidly at either end, because these areas are stable. The 'Neutral Zone' is a fluid place with no solid ground to walk on. This is exactly where Native American Contextual Ministry Movement found itself in the beginning, but now we are finally stepping to the other side and on to solid ground. In the 1990s we found ourselves breaking with older ministry patterns but not fully accepted by established churches. This is now changing. We were in the 'Neutral Zone' for a time but now we are seeing many new contextual ministries developing across the country. When we started some twenty years ago we were not taken very serious. Our critics were often educated at the doctoral level, and they did not value our perspective partly because our early leaders did not have an equal level of education. That has now changed, and today we are on our way to becoming a driving force in academic training for those wanting a theological education taught by Native contextual educators. Through this neutral zone, these leaders have maintained their focus on legitimizing a contextual perspective on evangelizing, disciple making, church planting, and other ministries.

This middle area of uncertainty can only be navigated by leaders who trust God and have seen where he is leading them. Manager-pastors find this zone scary because there is nothing solid to hold onto yet. This is the place where we need to hold tightly to God's hand and let him guide us through to the other side.

We will talk more about transition in the areas of emotional upsets, conflicts, leadership needs, saying goodbye to old methods, and 'developing a vision' in this half of the book. As you read on, I pray you will not feel overwhelmed but will hang in there and trust God to lead you.

Change and Emotions

As we begin to understand Christian ministry in the process of change and transition, we find there are no cookie-cutter methods that will work well for all groups. This is certainly true in Native American ministry. I have seen that Native churches need to start the change process at different levels – starting at whatever level they are on currently – according to their readiness to incorporate change.

My wife and I approached one Native church board to propose starting a contemporary service. We wanted to reach the younger crowd and the adults who were ready for a change. The current style used during the Sunday morning service had failed to reach these people. During our meeting, members voiced their concerns and asked questions. I imagined a meeting full of smiles and joy when the board heard that younger people were stepping forward to serve in the church. We thought they would be happy to see new ideas voiced and a vision for the lost reclaimed. What we experienced was more like a trial where we ended up defending ourselves. We had come to the meeting hoping to help this small Native church with outreach to the community. What we encountered was hesitation and suspicion of our vision. Bill Hybels calls this type of church environment 'A Vision-Free Environment'. He used this label when speaking of his childhood church where vision never had a chance.[2] Instead of offering their full support, we found the fear of change controlling their every move. The members valued their Sunday morning service over other avenues of outreach. For them to approve needed change was a very emotional and challenging undertaking. The 'Status quo' held them back and they have never pushed for change because they knew that to get their members to adjust their long-held habits would be too much work.[3] Even though we approached our proposal with logic and common sense, we failed to win solid approval. As a result, my wife and I were given their reluctant approval. Under such conditions, we withdrew our offer and later left the church in search of one willing to support our efforts. It was at this point that we found

---

[2] 'Leadership Summit', Willow Creek Community Church, South Barrington, IL, 2004.
[3] Rogers, *The Diffusion of Innovation*, p. 324.

ourselves attending Mesa View United Methodist Church in Albuquerque.

This is a common example of how preferences and habits thwart
change for the sake of keeping tradition alive. Even though we
sought to appeal to the membership logically and sensibly, we met
with various negative emotions. Change can be a controversial subject.

> When you suggest a change of habit, environment, relationship,
> or even spiritual direction, you are questioning each individual's
> personal preferences and the beliefs that back them. Even as
> Christian followers, we try to spiritualize our preferences, believ-
> ing that God is on our side and supportive of our opinions.[4]

Thus, Native churches over the years have considered their present
church methods – such as the older methods of revivals and camp
meetings – as the only way to 'do out-reach' and have sought to preserve their methods at all costs. They are promoting 'Churchianity'
rather than Christianity. It is important for us to remember that those
of us who are ready for change are in the minority. Most people are
content to remain where they are.

We came across another example of difficulty in proposing
change when my family and I were members of Fuller Avenue
Church of the Nazarene, an inner-city church in Grand Rapids,
Michigan. Fuller Avenue Church became aware of the seeker-sensi-
tive model of outreach used at Willow Creek Community Church in
Chicago, Illinois and tried to adopt this new approach. We took the
community survey suggested by Hybels to within a one-mile radius
of the church, even though most of the membership lived outside
this area. After gathering the data from the survey, we sat down to
analyze how best to implement the Willow Creek strategy. Incorporation of the Willow Creek model was too great a leap for the church.
The church was too entrenched in their older model. It was only
when we started to navigate the changes that we realized where the
members were in the level of readiness for change. In retrospect,
what we failed to do at Fuller Avenue Church was to make small,
incremental introductions toward bigger changes. The leadership was
ready, but the congregation was not. Eventually we gave up.

---

[4] Nelson and Appel, *How to Change Your Church*, p. 72.

What happened in these two churches? What made change so difficult? It was our failure to convince those who had emotional ties to the old ways, which made them unwilling to change. What can we do to understand the emotional side of change and avoid these struggles?

If I were to try to make the proposed changes again, I would work much more slowly and work at preparing the congregation more receptive for change. Implementing change at the Fuller Avenue Church became an emotional challenge. One major problem came from our older opinion leader. This leader influenced the older members to resist change. Rick Warren tells the story of one leader in the Nazarene denomination who noted, 'In the Nazarene church we do not have a Pope, but there is a little "pope" in each church'.[5] He was alluding to the older opinion leaders in each church. Unless we are able to get full support from theses opinion leaders, change will come hard. I must make a comment on this 'pope' issue. These 'popes' are in most denominational churches. The more familiar I become with the Native churches in the southwest, the more aware I am of the 'popes' in their congregations. I am seeing the influence they have over the established Native churches.

Robbins and Finley in their book, *Why Change Doesn't Work* share 'Seven Unchangeable Rules of Change'. The following are their rules adapted for our Native American churches:

1. Native American churches do what they feel is in their own best interest.

2. Native American churches are not inherently anti-change. Most will consider and embrace change if it has a positive meaning for them.

3. Native American people have a creative side, but when negatively stressed their creativity withers.

4. Native American people are diverse. No single solution will address all of their differences.

5. Native American churches believe in change after they see it work. For them, actions speak louder than words. With Native

---

[5] 'Purpose Driven Church Conference', 1997.

people outside the church there exists a deep-seated suspicion toward the Christian and toward change.

6. Native American churches must take ownership and picture what can happen in order to begin the change process. Then they must 'inhabit the vision' for it to come true and become permanent change.

7. Change must first be imagined. Unless it is imagined and engaged nothing will happen.[6]

These 'unchangeable rules of change' need to be understood and employed in a Native American setting if effective change is to happen. If you fail to take these seven tenets seriously, your work with Native American churches will fail. In the previous two illustrations, we not only see examples of how change attempts can hit the wall, but we also see people with different views and opinions about how change should happen. Just as the Body of Christ has individuals with different spiritual gifts and abilities, these same individuals are gifted to accept and respond to new ideas at different speeds. These differences are natural inclinations and do not make some people better or worse than others.[7] Understanding this valuable point will make implementation of change in any ministry easier.

What Does it all Mean?

So what do we do with the 'unchangeable rules of change' and our brief look at the types of people in our churches? For one thing, we must become aware of how change happens and also become aware of the people in our churches who can help us. I realize there is a negative side to all the data, but I want to take the most optimistic stance. Therefore, most of what I will share next has to do with the positive side of change.

Knowing the different types of people in our churches gives us a better appreciation for each of these groups. Each type contains believers in the Body of Christ. Each one is needed. I would like to

---

[6] Harvey Robbins and Michael Finley, *Why Change Doesn't Work* (Princeton, NJ: Peterson's, 1996), p. 52.

[7] Nelson and Appel, *How to Change Your Church*, p. 73.

share the strengths we can capitalize on in our efforts to introduce change, with some mention of the weaknesses of each type.

Even though we have many views and rates of acceptance of change, we can now better understand Rogers' description of five types of church members he calls the 'Adopters Categorizations: Innovators, Opinion leaders, Early adopters, Late adopters, and Resistant', as described in James White's book, *Rethinking the Church: A Challenge to Creative Redesign in an Age of Transition.*[8] These categories capture a sense of what I see in our Native American church members. Rogers explains how each type responds to change, transition, and new ideas. Every church has representatives of each type of each of the Innovations, Opinion Leaders, Early Adopters, Late Adopters and the Resistant.

Innovators

Innovators help us propose new ideas and approaches they believe can make us more effective – and to help us meet the changing needs of the future. Innovators are always at work. They represent from 2 to 5 percent of the average church membership. Some of their ideas can seem far-fetched, but we need them because they push the envelope of a stagnant status quo. Innovators look at life differently. They are easily bored by status quo thinking and thrive on introducing new ideas. Innovators tend to be intolerant of those who resist change. Innovators are the reason we need new 'Wineskins'.[9]

Innovators make change exciting. They are, as I like to refer to them 'Out of the box' thinkers. Innovators in the Native American Contextual Movement have stepped forward and become the vanguard, breaking new ground in Native American evangelism and ministry. These leaders in contextual ministry face the future with optimism and because they are the first to step forward, have had to take the brunt of the negative response to contextual ministry. They have managed to stay in the battle because of their divine calling.

Opinion Leaders

'Opinion leaders' are the progressives, some are open to change, and some are not. They are not the originators of new ideas, but when they see the positive side of change, they can act on it. When they

---

[8] White, *Rethinking the Church*, p. 145.
[9] White, *Rethinking the Church*, p. 142.

catch the vision, they are the main source for the implementation of change. They refine the new ideas into practical methods to keep up with changing times. Opinion leaders are accepted in their churches more than innovators are and are seen as more logical and safe. They embrace change only after they are convinced and, thereafter, are not threatened by it.

They are the ones who show their faith to others by moving ahead in an area of ministry not yet proven. Just like the innovators, they can be intolerant of those unwilling to change – those unwilling to venture into the 'promised land'. In addition, they can influence a church to resist change. Nevertheless, most times when handled with sensitivity, they can be our allies for change.[10] This group makes up from 10 to 20 percent of our church members. In either case these groups weigh the risk and then, in turn, can influence the acceptance or rejection of the Contextual Movement.

Early Adopters

'Early adopters' are the builders in the church. They give stability to new ideas and face the risks that come from giving up older ways. Early Adopters are not as resistant to change, but depend on the Opinion leaders to show them how they will benefit from the changes. They act as the 'settlers' after the Opinion leaders and In-novators have 'spied out the land'. They adapt new ideas and set models for application in place. The innovation can become the sense of identity gained from successful adaptation but they can become resistant when the application has a hard time making a fit.

Early Adopters may not move fast, but work better when they use incremental change and are valuable for carrying out change. They are viewed as level headed and stable. The Innovators are 'explorers', Opinion leaders the 'pioneers', and the Early adopters are the 'settlers'. While Innovators dream, Opinion leaders are busy figuring out practical ways to move forward. Early adopters carry out the ideas making them realistic.[11] This group makes up from 25 to 40 percent of Native church members.

---

[10] White, *Rethinking the Church*, p. 145.
[11] White, *Rethinking the Church*, p. 145.

Late Adopters

'Late Adopters' are those who would prefer not to change, but follow the crowd once the confusion is gone and all seems stable. Late Adopters help us remember our past and the values we treasure. Once on board, they become loyal to the new way of thinking after the Early adopters accept the new idea. On the plus side, their strong values are needed for stable growth. Their weakness is their inability to set up acceptable methods. This can cause them to lose perspective concerning the new changes.

Once Late adopters are on board, they keep us in balance. Innovators and Opinion leaders often see Late adopters as old fashioned, closed-minded, and resistant to change while they see themselves as adding strength to the future by preserving the past. Once we get the Late adopters in tune with what we are trying to do, they will become the backbone of our efforts.[12] Once the Late adopters become involved in the new approach, we then have nearly 90 percent of the Native church population involved, although the Late adopters themselves make up from 25 to 40 percent of our Native church members.

Resistant

The 'Resistant' do not want to change. They feel ministry should stay the same and the church should do ministry the way they have always done it. Although they only make up 16 percent, they seem much larger, because they make the most negative noise.[13]

They are an important group to add to the Contextual Movement, even though they are far from being Innovators. They are not bad people. Like the Judaizers in Paul the Apostle's day (Acts 15), they are sincere in their faith. Although misinformed, they believe God can only work through one method and that is their method.

Once the Resistant see how the other groups have accepted and faced their fears they will in fact concede to the Holy Spirit and accept that God is in the Contextual Movement. As the Resistant become more of a minority, they become less resistant and struggle to make the transition to being a contextual ministry. Their transition toward acceptance is an attempt to save face. What they do not realize is that others who have already made the transition want to come alongside

---

[12] White, *Rethinking the Church*, p. 146.
[13] White, *Rethinking the Church*, p. 146.

them and help them move forward in the cause of Christ. Still, their weakness will be their fear of the future. This can make them a 'thorn in the side' of a change agent. They can continue to be divisive while earnestly believing they are still right, making idols of their traditions and religious practices.[14]

The Apostles Paul's life was changed and thereafter he served God in a new contextual way. When the Resistant people in our churches accept that Jesus Christ is in the Contextual Movement, they too will have changed lives. The biggest benefit will be their understanding of the scriptures as now applied to contextual ministry. They will see that contextual ministry gives honor and respect to their past. Once the Resistant soften, they will need personal attention given with love and grace.

Summary

My goal within this section was to make you aware of the different categories that exist within our Native American population and churches. The Innovators and the Resistant will be the most visible. Most of the Native American people in the Early and Late adopter categories are waiting for the Opinion leader's decision – which will affect the future direction of Native ministries. You will find yourself in one of these categories and may find it difficult to accept those in other groups. I agree with this comment from Nelson and Appel:

> But because we have God's spirit in us, we make room for others' differences and appreciate what each brings to the table. Those less comfortable with change must recognize that God often in-troduces new things via more progressive brothers and sisters.[15]

Remember that the people within each group all love and serve Jesus Christ. Acts 1.8 says, 'You will be my witnesses'. This makes evangelism a human enterprise. We must figure out what will work best, all the while being guided by the Holy Spirit.

---

[14] White, *Rethinking the Church*, p. 146.
[15] Nelson and Appel, *How to Change Your Church*, p. 822.

5

LEADERSHIP NEEDED FOR CHANGE

When we step into the topic of leadership, we enter one of the most extensively researched fields in ministry. Rather than try to give you everything dealing with transition and change and its leadership requirements, I will highlight some of my own experiences with the transition process and those of some of my friends and colleagues. Transition and change in our Native churches is an area not well-traveled by writers. I will write about my personal views and integrate views that non-Native authors have encountered in similar situations.

We must better understand our need for appropriate leadership as the Native American Contextual Movement develops. Different styles of leadership work best depending on where a church is on the continuum of change. I want to describe the various styles on the continuum as applied to Native churches. These approaches are described by Nelson and Appel: Motivated/Unprepared, Partly Motivated/Partly Prepared, Motivated/Equipped, and Highly Motivated/Highly Equipped. The following are brief descriptions of each of the levels of readiness adapted for our context.

Motivated/Unprepared

These people are motivated to change, but unprepared for the process. This stage of readiness can work, but from my observation, it is not likely. When I first received my call to contextual ministry in 1992, God gave me the vision for contextual ministry, but I had to gain the experience and knowledge in order to be successful. What I learned over the next six years prepared me to start our contextual church in Grand Rapids Michigan. I was motivated, but I needed to take baby steps to the point of readiness. Occasionally, I have encountered individuals who have either read about or attended seminars or conferences taught by Richard Twiss or Randy Woodley.[1] The attendees believed that learning from these two leaders in contextual ministry qualified them to start and plant contextual ministries in their own communities. Without full preparation, these people are examples of the four types of soil Jesus spoke of in The Parable of the Sower (Matthew 13). In our application, the 'contextual seed' has been sown, but because these people have no 'roots' in contextual ministry experience, they make many mistakes and may fail, though supported by their leadership. I recommend that individuals in the Motivated/Unprepared category deliberately slow down even though they are motivated. They need to take the time to study contextual ministry from the few individuals who have weathered the storms in their contextual-learning journeys. In a city or on a rural reservation, poorly-prepared people can cause many problems for others who are doing similar ministry in the same communities. By making a few critical mistakes in contextual implementation they can set other ministries' achievements back many years. Motivated/Unprepared people are in all ministries. We all know individuals who can be described by the phrase, 'They have enough knowledge or information to be dangerous'. An example of the trouble that can be caused by the Motivated/Unprepared took place in 2001 when the Rio Grande Conference of the United Methodist Church backed a ministry effort to explore the possibilities of a ministry start in Albuquerque, New Mexico among the Native Americans. This initiative had the support and blessing of the churches. The leader was apparently highly motivated for this project but lacked the practical understanding for church planting, not to mention the contextual understanding for urban Native American ministry. After three years attempting to accomplish this task, there was no ministry in place and no further ministry was organized. As of today, there has not been another effort to start a contextual congregation.

---

[1] The late Dr. Richard Twiss was president of Wiconi International. http://www.wiconi.com. Dr. Randy Woodley is Professor of Faith and Culture and Director of Intercultural and Indigenous Studies at George Fox University in Newberg, OR.

Partly Motivated/Partly Prepared

A good example of a partly motivated and partly prepared ministry is the Brethren in Christ Navajo mission in Farmington, New Mexico. The staff and new director there had just come on board and were ready to make some changes. They knew something had to be different but they did not know what to do or how to go about making the changes.

Most Native American ministries find themselves in this stage of readiness. These individuals often know their own limited readiness. They spend the time preparing themselves to do a better job as ministry windows open in their communities. I have encountered two such ministries in New Mexico. First Nations Fellowship in Farmington is led by Pastor Duane Bristow. He is non-Native, but he realizes that limitation. He has caught the vision and has, with the help of the Native membership, developed one of the better contextual ministries in the region. This pastor has taken the time to learn from the few more experienced leaders in contextual ministry and has had great results. The second one is the Vineyard Church in Chaparral led by Pastor Ernie Neria and is a good example of a Partly motivated/Partly prepared ministry. This group spent the time to gain as much knowledge and personal mentoring in order to make the greatest impact in their community, making minimal mistakes. Their willingness to take the time to prepare is proving them successful in their attempts to contextualize their ministry. They realize the full implication of doing contextual ministry in their rural area. They are heading in the right direction by keeping their motivation high and continually increasing their readiness by attending every seminar and conference their group is able to attend. They have plans in the future to host a Powwow in their area as a way to reach into the Native community. I look forward to this initiative because I have been asked to help them organize it.

Motivated/Equipped

Motivated and equipped people in ministry have the desire to see new styles of Native ministry develop, and they have spent the time preparing with people who have the vision to make change happen. Few have made it to this stage, but those who have are setting the pace for others. Richard Twiss was one of these leaders and led the way for all of us to follow. He advanced contextual ministry using the open door God gave him through the release of his books and his extensive speaking schedule. Veteran leaders like Richard and others have had the privilege of creating awareness in the larger church – creating awareness of the need for Native approaches to Native evangelism. Richard's unique position gave others the encouragement needed to continue in the face of opposition. His 'Many Nations One Voice' conferences were very popular and well attended. Because of Richard's ministry, the strongholds Satan has over the minds of many older – and some younger Native pastors are being broken. **Some of these Native pastors had bought into the lie that our Native cultures are evil and only white European cultural ways can be Christian.**

After six years of study and prayer, a team of people and I in Grand Rapids set out to start a unique style of 'doing church' with Native Americans – a style which reflected the identity of the local Natives. The people God pulled together, and these church plants were motivated and well equipped. Each person on the team brought a needed part of the Body of Christ to the effort. Before the start date, I had prepared for this task by studying the Native religions of the area and by building trust and relationships with the Native community. I did this by working on local Powwow committees, being involved in the local Indian education program, and other local Native American congregations' programs. Before starting the new ministry in Grand Rapids, my wife and I had a house church for two years, attended by a few of the local community members. We incorporated contextual ministry methods. Because of our presence in the community, local Natives who did not attend our house church would ask us to pray for their local community concerns. Further, part of my calling to ministry was to prepare myself academically, receiving a Bachelor of Science degree in anthropology. I had just started seminary at the Grand Rapids Theological Seminary when God brought us all together for this church plant. Just as God used Richard Twiss in a unique up-front role; he has used my wife and me in a similar fashion at the lesser-known grass roots ministry level. We

have progressed from our Motivated/Equipped stage in Grand Rapids to an open door for more contextual awareness within the Native
ministries in the southwest where we now reside.

Highly Motivated/Highly Equipped

In this setting, the ministry leaders desire to make changes; they are
educated in contextual approaches; and they are prepared to implement what they have learned. Only a handful of people progress to
this stage. Those who make it to this level have weathered many
storms, have sometimes tried and failed, but have never lost the vision to which God has called them. Randy and Edith Woodley are
one such couple. For over two decades Randy Woodley has led the
way toward the understanding and implementation of contextual
thought and ministry. Randy and Edith are the 'vanguard' in contextual ministry and are leaders I have had the privilege of following.
His unique ministry call was to start the Eloheh Village for Indigenous Leadership and Ministry Development near Wilmore, Kentucky. Their ministry continues now in Oregon, where Randy has
taken his unique ministry style to a new level as a professor at George
Fox University in Newberg, Oregon. Randy has authored many
books, furthering the cause of contextual ministry.

Kyle and Marcia Taylor are another influential couple who have
become firm in their belief in contextual ministry while walking out
their journey of faith. At first they were not sure if contextual ministry was of God. They started a unique approach to contextual ministry they call Common Ground, taken from 2 Cor. 2.29. God has
given them many open doors through which to spread the awareness
of contextual ministry and to gain a network of supporters. The Tay-
lors are on staff at Bacone College in Muskogee, Oklahoma. Kyle is
on the board of Wiconi International in Vancouver, Washington.
Highly motivated/Highly equipped leaders do not just arise from
among the veterans of contextual ministry; they develop from the
trenches. God can raise up leaders from any level on the continuum
if they are willing to follow his leading.

Managers and Leaders

Manager Pastors maintain and try to keep their ministries running smoothly. When change is not a consideration, Manager (managing) pastors will do. Manager Pastors have been maintaining the status quo for too long. Churches with these kinds of pastors desperately need change. They are stuck in an ineffective mode. However, they are not completely ineffective. The evangelism style taught to them by non-Native ministries has 'managed' to bring some into the kingdom. There is a dire need for change if the untold thousands of Native Americans disaffected with the white man's church and its image of Jesus are to be reached. The model of church identity – as only residing in the white man's culture – is well established in our present Native churches. But God is ready to make some changes which will require not manager pastors but leader pastors. Nelson and Appel describe leadership as the following:

> We refer to the process by which change issues are initiated by people of influence within and among groups ... not all influence is leadership, but leadership is the special kind of influence that significantly affects decision making, direction setting and speed ... leaders are people who create, manage, and develop change within groups.[2]

The Nelson and Appel description of leadership deals directly with change, the changes we face in the Native Contextual Movement. To change the status quo will take decision making, direction setting, and the appropriate pace needed to create, manage, and develop new contextual ministries.

These results can be obtained in many ways. Robbins and Finley describe four leadership approaches used to produce change. They call these approaches 'Pummel', 'Pamper', 'Push', and 'Pull'. They write that 'Pummel' is a strong approach that uses manipulation and emotional pressure. 'Pamper' is a nonthreatening approach, with a hands-off leadership style that lets people do whatever they want. 'Push' is a bullying approach which uses fear and pain, mostly to avoid unnecessary pain. 'Pull', which is the one I recommend, says, 'Do what you must do in order to achieve the future you dream

---

[2] Nelson and Appel, *How to Change Your Church*, p. 101.

about'. 'Pull' is an approach used to motivate people using positive motivators. Robbins and Finley suggest that change brought about by using 'Pull' produces long-term change because people do not feel manipulated. Instead, 'Pull' creates the vision for a better life. Seeing their dreams realized is a powerful motivator. Leaders who use 'Pull', will create, manage, and develop change more easily because those who are led feel they are a part of the process.[3]

There is much that can be said about leadership during the process of change. I realize I am only touching the surface. I hope what I have shared so far will benefit you and motivate you to start the process of change in your own ministry. Finally, I want to share several points Nelson and Appel make. They point out what leaders can do to start learning about change toward contextual ministry. The following are their points adapted for contextual needs:

1. Immerse yourself in books on leadership and change.

2. Learn how to get opinion leaders in your corner.

3. Form a team in your church.

4. Take your team to contextual ministries like the Brethren in Christ in Farmington, New Mexico

5. Make it a point to attend one of the yearly symposiums presented by the North American Institute for Indigenous Theological Studies. These symposiums are held in June each year.

6. Have your opinion leaders read this book and others listed in the bibliography.

7. Design a retreat where topics of change and transition can be brainstormed.

8. Bring in a consultant to help you work through change strategies – or invite one of the leaders in Native contextual ministry to speak to your group.

9. Prepare a message to preach on the biblical foundation for contextual ministry which includes: facing their fears, faith and risk, and how God does the new.

---

[3] Robbins and Finley, *Why Change Doesn't Work*, p. 19.

10. Take your opinion leaders through a study series using Nelson and Appel's *How to Change Your Church without Killing It* or Dan Southerlands' *Transitioning*, both of which are excellent books for helping congregations navigate change.

11. Lastly and most importantly, attend the Wiconi Family Camp in Turner, Oregon. This camp is a living laboratory on how to live out contextual life and ministry.[4]

---

[4] Nelson and Appel, *How to Change Your Church*, p. 101.

6

CONCLUDING THOUGHTS FOR EMERGING LEADERS

We are living in an age of computer technology. If you are like me, you continue to learn as much as you can each year just to keep up with the basics. This can hold true in grasping the knowledge needed to venture into contextual ministry as well. In spite of computer technology, you can keep using your typewriter, encyclopedia, and snail mail; or you can learn word processing, the internet, email, Facebook, and much more to stay relevant. The same is true in ministry. It is easy to stay in an older model, but it will take time and effort to become familiar with all the facets involved in contextual ministry. If you want to be on the cutting edge of ministry, you must become a contextual learner.

My wife and I have promoted awareness and empowered leaders in new ways of contextual ministry in Grand Rapids, Albuquerque, and Farmington. We have since started other contextual ministries with the Immersion Class in South Dakota, and we are planning other initiatives in Iowa and in North Carolina.

To Pastors

Making the necessary changes toward becoming a contextual ministry takes courage, perseverance, and patience. I have weathered many storms in order to 'stay in the race'. I have learned that establishing true change is much more involved than starting out on a whim and trying a few new approaches just because they seem 'neat' or 'cool'.

Nelson and Appel say, 'Do not institute change unless you are sure God has called you to it. Only vision-called people should take the risk of disrupting a faith community',[1] which applying contextual ministry approaches will do. If you believe this is your calling, use the information in this book to move boldly into the future.

Pastors, too much is at stake when we are dealing with the eternal destiny of unreached Native American people. God has called us to do his will in the context of our local churches. Always remember that every church has problems with change. When you go back to your churches fired up with new ideas after attending a conference you will likely face resistance. The Bible is full of stories of leaders who faced problems and criticism. One important lesson I have learned – and you may have too – is that no matter what you do, you will never make everyone happy. When I face criticism from church members or from denominational leaders, I remember to pray for those who persecute me.

One crucially important reality that keeps me persisting as a leader in these transitional times is the fact that those around me in my Native Community need Jesus Christ. We have a great responsibility. We cannot continue to do ministry the way we used to, because the Native Americans today are different. They do not have a foundational knowledge of the Bible, and their values have changed with each generation. They have grown further away from biblical knowledge and the church. This is why you as a leader must promote change and transition toward contextual ministry styles in our Native Churches.

To Those in the Pew

You are the 'critical mass' needed for the Contextual Movement to forge ahead. Right or wrong, you and others in the pew can hold your church back, or you can lend support to those in leadership who are making the decisions that may bring thousands into the Kingdom. We need you to come alongside your pastors and lay leaders in order to give them the motivation to dream new dreams and lead your local Native churches into this exciting new season. Partner with your pastor and become one of the many Native churches stepping out in faith to become contextual churches. When your leaders want to

---

[1] Nelson and Appel, *How to Change Your Church*, p. 316.

make changes and you are unsure of how to respond, remember that God wants you to follow your leaders. The scriptures say, 'Obey your leaders and submit to their authority. They keep watch over you as those who must give an account. Obey them so that their work will be a joy, not a burden, for that would be of no advantage to you' (Heb. 13.14).

It takes time to understand what is taking place. I had two Aunties who, for my first few years in contextual ministry, prayed that I would be delivered from contextual ministry. These two women went to their graves with these prayers. Now they are in heaven sitting with my father and mother, who I can imagine are saying to them, 'I told you he was doing God's will'. It took my mother six years to admit that she could see what God was doing. Then she became my biggest supporter and prayer warrior. In the book of Acts a Pharisee named Gamaliel spoke up to those persecuting the disciples with these words:

> Leave these men alone! Let them go! For if their purpose or ac-
> tivity is of human origin, it will fail but if it is from God you will
> not be able to stop these men; you will only find yourself fighting
> against God (Acts 5.32-35).

To Lay Leaders

The 'promised land' for your church is not far away. Just as the spies who entered it came back with differing opinions of the same land, lay leadership also view changes and especially contextual changes with varied views. Caleb and Joshua saw the potential; others will only see the problems. Your opinions and views can make or break your pastoral leadership. When you finally see the land 'flowing with milk and honey' you need to let your pastor know it. Your encouragement can make all the difference. Your influence not only affects your pastor, but also other members of your congregation. How you deal with implementing change can be the momentum needed to make change and transition a reality.

Further, as lay leaders you can count yourself privileged to be at this exciting time in church history. If you had the opportunity to speak with God and he gave you the opportunity to be placed in one of the most important seasons in church history, he would very likely put you here. He has opened the door to make the greatest difference for the Kingdom. He wants to position you right where you are because we are on the verge of one of the most dynamic times in history. God has also given others his vision for new dimensions of ministry opportunity. He wants to place you strategically in the lives of Native people who need him, but they will only come through an approach sensitive to their context. You can be like Esther and fulfill God's plan in 'such a time as this '(Est. 4.14). You can advance God's work in your ministry through a Native church that is culturally sensitive and bold enough to risk change and leave behind decades of ineffective evangelistic styles.

Every time God has moved in a new direction, there have been those who are among the first to cross the line and go where God wants to lead them. They usually receive this direction before the majority of other believers. If you are one of these people, keep the faith, hold your course, and be among those who step across the line – enjoy your front row seat. For years to come, people will benefit from your up-front and behind-the-scenes labor of love.[2] I pray you will be inspired by these words as I have been.

Summary

During the Saddleback Community Church seminar, Rick Warren shared the following statement, 'If you always do what you've always done, you'll always get what you've always got'.[3] His statement may sound cute, but it resounds with truth. Albert Einstein said the definition of insanity is doing something over and over again and expecting a different result.

This has been the way we have approached Native American ministry in the past. Each year we have started out with goals, new plans, and strategies to make a bigger impact for the Kingdom of God. We have put new names on our old programs, created new colorful brochures, and added different staff. What we failed to change were the basic values and the philosophy of our old, outdated programs; and we expect different results each year – and each year we receive the

---

[2] Nelson and Appel, *How to Change Your Church*, p. 316.
[3] 'Purpose Driven Church Conference', 1997.

same pathetic results. We have done this all in the name of clinging to our traditional methods and mind-sets.

We began with the analogy of classic car restoration. Our tendency is to hold onto the 'classic' from the past, trying to maintain the appearance of a finely-tuned modern machine. People may be sincere in their efforts, but they continue year after year insisting on their preferred methods. By doing this they are saying that a generation of Native American people 'can go to Hell'. Underlying this is an attitude that says, 'What I believe is right is far more important than experiencing what you say God is blessing'. So year after year we plug away, satisfied with 'declining' or 'plateau' churches while the Native American population in need of Jesus is growing larger each year.

I have tried within these pages to give you the basic information you need to gain the courage to break from the past, move forward, and make needed changes. In this way, many Native American people can come into the kingdom without denying who God made them to be. I realize many of you are caught in difficult situations, feeling the pressure from a few who are set on clinging to the status quo – while you want to break out and risk making changes. The thought of going against the grain by risking association with those more progressive contextual leaders is frightening and is holding you back. Therefore, I ask you, whom are you trying to please, men or God? God has shown a few leaders just how big he can be and that he is able to do far more than we can imagine. I want to encourage those of you who want to please God to press toward the mark of the higher calling. I have faced the problems you are foreseeing and have stayed in the race. When you choose to follow God 'who is making a way in the desert' (Isa. 43.19) you may risk losing friendships with members of the old guard, but you will also gain many more friends and fellow servants who are leading the way in a new direction. Who knows, some of the old guard may follow your lead and risk change too – because you did.

If you are ready to step out and make the needed changes, I welcome you.

Let's all enjoy the ride!

ABOUT THE AUTHOR

Casey Church

(*Ankwawango*)

Hole in the Clouds

I am a Pokagon Band Potawatomi Indian from southwest Lower Michigan. My Indian name is *Ankwawango*, which means 'Hole in the Clouds'. My personal experience in cross-cultural ministry has not led me to other lands. It has led me to develop cross-cultural ministries among Native Americans here in the United States where there are over five hundred Native tribes and over 250 language groups. Since my calling to this ministry, I have worked with several tribes in a pan tribal method and approach. Most Native American people have assimilated into the white culture to varying degrees. I have had to live in two worlds: the Native American traditional world and the Christian church world – which has been heavily influenced by white missionaries and pastors. I believe my personal background has uniquely prepared me for developing a cross-cultural evangelism that can effectively reach Native North Americans. I have also married cross-culturally. My wife Lora is a Navajo who was raised in Albuquerque, New Mexico. Although we are both Native Americans, we come from two very different cultural traditions. We have five children and live in Albuquerque.

I grew up in a Native community in Lower Michigan and attended a small Native United Methodist Church. My Christian parents made church a priority in our family life. We always had trouble keeping our church life separate from our Native-community life. My pastor was my Uncle, the Rev. Lewis White Eagle Church. In our community, he also had to walk the delicate balance required by living in two worlds. I was keenly aware of this unnatural separation in our lives, but still felt a call to become involved in Native Christian ministry. In 1988 I accepted God's call and dedicated my life to serving Him. It was not until spring of 1992 that God visited me in a dream/vision and helped bring unity to these two unique worlds. As a result, I now live a life that dares to combine these two traditions into one seamless expression of Christ's love in order to reach my own people.

Through this unexpected calling, God has led me down the path of studying both traditions. In this way I work to help our Native people realize that their traditions do not have to be separated from their life with Christ – as they have been taught by both Native and non-Native missionaries and pastors. The task of learning both traditions is challenging, but I believe Christ has helped me to see that one can incorporate the good and honorable aspects of Native culture into authentic expressions of Christian praise and worship to the Father, Son, and Holy Spirit.

After this revelation, I became involved in planting Native contextual ministries. These were places where God could be worshiped within the context and worldview of urban Native Americans. I have also studied under Native traditional elders and attended Grand Rapids Theological Seminary and Fuller Theological Seminary. I have become steeped in contextual theologizing both from my own personal experience and from my graduate studies. These two avenues of learning have helped me in ministry. In have now completed my Doctor in Intercultural Studies degree at Fuller's School of Intercultural Studies.

Since my dream/vision in 1992, I have sought to develop culturally appropriate methods of prayer and worship from within the framework of a Native American worldview. Native American Christian spiritual leaders have mentored me. They have taught me how to conduct ceremonies and rituals that honor God as well as Native culture. In addition to their counsel I have earned a degree in Anthropology from Grand Valley State University in Michigan and a Master of Arts in Inter-cultural Studies and a Doctor of Inter-cultural Studies from Fuller Theological Seminary.

I have continued to maintain a personal involvement with the Native American community in Albuquerque while working on my seminary degree. At Fuller I have learned to incorporate culturally appropriate expressions of worship, which I feel, will free Native American people to more fully understand the Creator from within their Native worldview. I believe God has chosen me for this ministry because I am an insider and can better adapt Western theological training to the traditional Native American context.

I have applied this unique ministry model to Native evangelism and developed two contextual ministries that have borne good fruit. Many people have encouraged me to continue my education and to develop a theology that is fully Native American. Through my ministry and my education I hope to write a theology of prayer and develop other contextual material from a Native American point of view as well as train and mentor the emerging generation of Native American leaders. These new leaders will ultimately reach the Native people of whom only 5 percent claim to be Christians.

I am not fluent in any Native language including my own, Potawatomi. Our Native people were taught by white missionaries and government programs to forget our languages so that we might be more fully assimilated into white culture. This perspective has been prevalent across all of North America, especially in the urban areas. Like many Native people, I have learned English, but I believe it will be of great value because I am called to reach urban Native Americans where English is widely used. The urban Natives are rapidly losing their languages with each generation – even where I live in the southwest where isolation has, in the past, helped to preserve languages and culture. I have been to several Native church services where attempts have been made to use both a Native language and English. This combination is a hindrance to the growth of Native churches in my opinion.

I have pastored a contextual Native American church plant in Grand Rapids, Michigan, and now in Albuquerque, New Mexico. My wife and I also led The Soaring Eagle Ministry, which promoted contextual ministry awareness. Through Soaring Eagle I pastored a contextual ministry and hosted a prayer circle in our home for Native American community members and sponsored conferences on contextual ministry at our original home church, Mesa View United Methodist Church in Albuquerque. Soaring Eagle no longer meets and I have devoted most of my ministry time to working with the Brethren in Christ Overcomers alcohol treatment program in Farmington, New Mexico. I am a board member with the North American Institute for Indigenous Theological Studies (NAIITS) and am a contributing writer for its academic journal and a workshop presenter at its symposiums. Finally, I am now the Director of Wiconi International, based in Vancouver, Washington. This style of contextual ministry was founded by the late Dr. Richard Twiss (Sicangu Lakota) and his wife Katherine.

Despite the many challenges of working in this type of ministry, my wife and I are excited about the great potential that exists to call out a new generation of Native Americans who will love and follow Jesus and share him in such a way that many Native people will rise up and say, 'This is good news!' To that end we live and to that end we serve.

BIBLIOGRAPHY

Allen, R., *Missionary Methods: St. Paul's or Ours?* (Grand Rapids, MI: Eerdmans, 1996).

American Heritage Dictionary (Boston, MA: Houghton Mifflin, 1985).

Anderson, L., *Dying for Change* (Minneapolis, MN: Bethany House Publishers, 1990).

Barna, G., *The Second Coming of the Church* (Nashville, TN: Word, 1998).

Barna, G., *Grow Your Church from the Outside In* (Ventura, CA: Regal Books, 2002).

Barna, G. and F. Viola, *Pagan Christianity: Exploring the Roots of Our Church Practices* (Carol Stream, IL: Tyndale Momentum, 2008).

Bridges, W., *Managing Transition* (Reading, MA: Perseus Books, 1991).

Chand, S., *Futuring: Leading Your Church into Tomorrow* (Grand Rapids, MI: Baker Books, 2002).

Donovan, V., *Christianity Rediscovered* (Maryknoll, NY: Orbis Books, 2005).

Hybels, B., *Courageous Leadership* (Grand Rapids, MI: Zondervan, 2002).

Kotter, J., *Leading Change* (Boston, MA: Harvard Business School Press, 1996).

Kraft, C., *Anthropology for Christian Witness* (Maryknoll, NY: Orbis Books, 1996).

Malphurs, A., *Pouring New Wine into Old Wineskins: How to Change a Church Without Destroying It* (Grand Rapids, MI: Baker Books, 1997).

Nelson, Allen and Gene Appel, *How to Change Your Church Without Killing It* (Grand Rapids, MI: Zondervan, 2000).

Quinn, R., *Deep Change* (San Francisco, CA: Jossey-Bass, 1996).

Regale, M., *Death of the Church* (Grand Rapids, MI: Zondervan, 1995).

Richardson, R., *Evangelism Outside the Box* (Downers Grove, IL: InterVarsity Press, 2000).

Robbins, H. and M. Finley, *Why Change Doesn't Work* (Princeton, NJ: Peterson's, 1996).

Rogers, E., *The Diffusion of Innovation* (New York, NY: The Free Press, 1995).

Roland, A., *Missionary Methods: St. Paul's or Ours?* (Grand Rapids, MI: Eerdmans, 1996).

Schaller, L., *The Change Agent* (Nashville, TN: Abindon Press, 1972).

Smith, C., *White Man's Gospel* (Winnipeg, Manitoba: Indian Life Books, 1997).

Southerland, D., *Transitioning: Leading Your Church Through Change* (Grand Rapids, MI: Zondervan, 2002).

Twiss, R., *One Church Many Tribes* (Ventura, CA: Regal Books, 2000).

White, J., *Rethinking the Church: A Challenge to Creative Redesign in an Age of Transition* (Grand Rapids, MI: Baker Books, 2003).

Woodley, R., *Living in Color* (Grand Rapids, MI: Chosen Books, 2001).

Index of Biblical References

Index of Authors

Wiconi
Removing Barriers, Building Bridges

Learn more about Wiconi,

Wiconi
P.O. Box5246
Vancouver, WA 98668

Email: office@wiconi.com
Phone: 360-607-2599

Web site: www.wiconi.com

Made in the USA
Monee, IL
24 June 2024

60441075R00049